# LOOK ALIVE TWENTY-FIVE

CW01643252

## BY JANET EVANOVICH

### THE STEPHANIE PLUM NOVELS

*One for the Money*

*Two for the Dough*

*Three to Get Deadly*

*Four to Score*

*High Five*

*Hot Six*

*Seven Up*

*Hard Eight*

*To the Nines*

*Ten Big Ones*

*Eleven on Top*

*Twelve Sharp*

*Lean Mean Thirteen*

*Fearless Fourteen*

*Finger Lickin' Fifteen*

*Sizzling Sixteen*

*Smokin' Seventeen*

*Explosive Eighteen*

*Notorious Nineteen*

*Takedown Twenty*

*Top Secret Twenty-One*

*Tricky Twenty-Two*

*Turbo Twenty-Three*

*Hardcore Twenty-Four*

*Look Alive Twenty-Five*

THE FOX AND O'HARE NOVELS WITH LEE GOLDBERG

*The Heist*

*The Chase*

*The Job*

*The Scam*

*The Pursuit*

KNIGHT AND MOON

*Curious Minds* (with Phoef Sutton)

*Dangerous Minds*

THE LIZZY AND DIESEL NOVELS

*Wicked Appetite*

*Wicked Business*

*Wicked Charms* (with Phoef Sutton)

THE BETWEEN THE NUMBERS STORIES

*Visions of Sugar Plums*

*Plum Lovin'*

*Plum Lucky*

*Plum Spooky*

THE ALEXANDRA BARNABY NOVELS

*Metro Girl*

*Motor Mouth*

*Troublemaker* (graphic novel)

# LOOK ALIVE TWENTY-FIVE

A STEPHANIE PLUM NOVEL

Janet Evanovich

G. P. PUTNAM'S SONS · NEW YORK

PUTNAM

G. P. Putnam's Sons
*Publishers Since 1838*
An imprint of Penguin Random House LLC
375 Hudson Street
New York, New York 10014

Copyright © 2018 by Evanovich, Inc.
Penguin supports copyright. Copyright fuels creativity, encourages diverse voices, promotes free speech, and creates a vibrant culture. Thank you for buying an authorized edition of this book and for complying with copyright laws by not reproducing, scanning, or distributing any part of it in any form without permission. You are supporting writers and allowing Penguin to continue to publish books for every reader.

Library of Congress Cataloging-in-Publication Data

Names: Evanovich, Janet, author.
Title: Look alive twenty-five / Janet Evanovich.
Description: New York : G. P. Putnam's Sons, an imprint of Penguin Random House LLC, [2018] | Series: A Stephanie Plum Novel ; 25
Identifiers: LCCN 2018038157| ISBN 9780399179228 (hardcover) | ISBN 9780399179235 (ePub)
Subjects: | BISAC: FICTION / Mystery & Detective / Women Sleuths. | FICTION / Humorous. | GSAFD: Mystery fiction. | Humorous fiction.
Classification: LCC PS3555.V2126 L66 2018 | DDC 813/.54—dc23
LC record available at https://lccn.loc.gov/2018038157

International edition ISBN: 9780525540199

Printed in the United States of America
1 3 5 7 9 10 8 6 4 2

Book design by Amy Hill

This is a work of fiction. Names, characters, places, and incidents either are the product of the author's imagination or are used fictitiously, and any resemblance to actual persons, living or dead, businesses, companies, events, or locales is entirely coincidental.

# CHAPTER ONE

VINCENT PLUM BAIL Bonds is one of several storefront businesses on Hamilton Avenue in Trenton, New Jersey. It's run by my cousin Vinnie and owned by his wiseguy father-in-law, Harry the Hammer. Connie Rosolli is the office manager. My name is Stephanie Plum, and my official title is bond enforcement agent. I'm assisted by Lula. We're not sure exactly what Lula does, and we've never been able to come up with a title for her.

Connie, Lula, and I were looking out the big plate glass window at a Chevy Bolt parked at the curb. It was a small car overstuffed with large women.

"Do you know who's in that car?" Lula asked Connie.

"Madam Zaretsky, Vinnie's dominatrix, is driving," Connie

said. "Little Sally, his happy endings masseuse, is next to her. It's hard to see who's in the back seat, but it might be his bookie."

"Vinnie has a lady bookie?" Lula asked.

"She used to be a man," Connie said, "but Vinnie stayed with her through the transition."

"Good for him," Lula said. "He's always been open-minded anyways. He didn't even care what sex that duck was."

The women got out of the car and marched into the office. Madam Zaretsky had jet-black hair pulled back in a bun. Her lipstick was blood red. Her nails were creepy long and matched her lips. She was wearing a black bandage dress and spike-heeled black pumps. Little Sally wasn't all that little. She was a plump five-five with a lot of frizzy red hair, an abundance of boob, and legs like tree trunks. The bookie was almost seven feet tall in heels. She was tastefully dressed in a pale-yellow sheath dress and patent nude pumps. Her makeup was understated. Her hands were big enough to palm a basketball, and she had gym monkey muscles.

"Whoa," Lula whispered to me. "That's a big bookie."

"Where is he?" Zaretsky said. "We need to talk to him. He owes us money."

"He's not here," Connie said. "Can I help you?"

"Sure, he's here," Lula said. "He's in his office."

The bonds office consists of a reception area with Connie's desk and some uncomfortable seating choices. Vinnie's private lair is off to one side, and a large storeroom stretches across the back of the building.

The three women sashayed over to Vinnie's office, but before they reached his door I heard Vinnie throw the bolt to lock them out.

"I know you're in there, Vinnie," Zaretsky said. "Open the door."

Silence. Vinnie wasn't answering.

*"Vinnie!"* Zaretsky said. "Open this door or Sally is going to kick it in."

"Makes sense," Lula said. "Sally's the one in combat boots. You don't want to kick a door down wearing Louboutins. You could ruin them doing something like that."

Sally gave the door a good kick with her boot heel, but the door didn't budge.

"Stand back," Zaretsky said.

She took a silver-plated Glock out of her handbag and squeezed off a shot. The round ricocheted off the door and took out Connie's desk lamp.

"His door's got a steel core," Connie said.

Zaretsky put her gun back into her bag. "You tell that weasel we want our money."

Connie gathered up the desk lamp pieces. "I'll pass it along."

"C'mon, girls," Zaretsky said. "We have better things to do than to hang here all day."

Zaretsky motioned for no one to say anything, and the women flattened themselves against the wall on either side of the door.

After a couple minutes, Vinnie opened the door a crack. "Are they gone?" he asked.

The women pushed the door open and stormed into the inner office. Vinnie shrieked and tried to scramble around his desk, but the bookie grabbed him.

"I haven't got any money," Vinnie said. "I swear to God, I'll pay you when I get some money."

In a very ladylike fashion, the bookie wrapped her hands around Vinnie's ankles and effortlessly held him upside down about a foot off the floor.

Vinnie is five foot nine and slim. His black hair is slicked back and wouldn't move in hurricane-force winds. His pants are narrow-legged and tight across his butt. His shirts are shiny and fit like skin. His complexion is Mediterranean. His dick has an adventuresome spirit and is most likely hideously diseased.

The bookie shook Vinnie up and down as if he was trying to empty Vinnie's pockets, but Vinnie's pants were too tight for anything to fall out.

"Tell Connie to give you the petty cash," Vinnie said. "It's all I've got."

The bookie dropped Vinnie, and the three women went to Connie.

"I've got two hundred and twenty dollars here," Connie said. "Sign this receipt."

Zaretsky signed the receipt and took the cash. "This isn't nearly enough," she shouted to Vinnie. "We expect payment in full by the end of the week, or we're going to your wife. And until you pay up you're cut off from services."

The women turned, huffed out of the office, got into the little car, and sped off.

"How old do you think Madam Zaretsky is?" Lula asked.

"She's in her sixties," Connie said. "Vinnie's been with her for a long time."

"She's in good shape," Lula said. "She's got excellent biceps. Must be from all that whipping she does."

Vinnie was on his feet. "What the hell were you thinking?" he yelled at Lula. "Why did you tell them I was in my office?"

"You need to pay the ladies," Lula said. "It's not good to stiff service providers. And you better shape up, because Madam Zaretsky said she was going to your wife next."

"Maybe if you two loser enforcers would actually make a capture I could pay the ladies," Vinnie said. "It's like I'm running a charity bailout here. How about if you stop snarfing those donuts on Connie's desk and make a feeble attempt to haul in Victor Waggle. Is that too much to ask?"

"How about if I rearrange your face so your nose is in the back of your head?" Lula said.

Vinnie closed his door and slid the bolt.

"Who's Victor Waggle?" Lula asked Connie.

"Failed to appear for court on Friday. High bond. Nutcase. Stabbed two people on State Street and urinated on their dog."

"That's a terrible thing to do," Lula said. "It's not nice to urinate on a dog. I hope that dog's okay. What kind of dog was it?"

"Shih tzu," Connie said.

"What about the people?" I asked.

"They'll live," Connie said.

"Motive?" I asked.

"Waggle said he was having a bad day."

Connie handed his file to me, and I paged through it. Photo of a guy with crazy bugged-out eyes and punked-up hair. Twenty-three years old. Eye color red. Hair color black. Had a tattoo of a snake coiled around his neck.

"Did anyone else come in?" I asked Connie.

"Annie Gurky didn't show for court on Friday. She's a low bond. Shoplifting while drunk and disorderly. And Wayne Kulicki. Eat and Go shorted him on his fries, so he destroyed the place."

"I've been shorted on fries there too," Lula said. "It's the drive-thru window. They always screw you over at the drive-thru window."

Connie handed me the two additional files, and I organized all three in order of difficulty. I'd go after Annie Gurky first, Wayne Kulicki second, and hope Victor Waggle got run over by a truck before I started searching for him.

Vinnie popped out of his office again. "And don't forget about the deli."

"Deli?" I asked.

Vinnie narrowed his eyes at Connie. "Didn't you tell them about the deli?"

"I was getting to it," Connie said.

"Well, get to it faster," Vinnie said. "It's not gonna run itself."

Vinnie retreated back into his office.

Lula and I looked over at Connie.

"You remember Ernie Sitz," Connie said. "He skipped out on a racketeering charge last year."

"He's still in the wind," I said. "The rumor is that he's in South America somewhere."

Connie nodded. "One of his many businesses was Red River Deli. He used it as collateral on his bond, and two weeks ago Vincent Plum Bail Bonds was awarded ownership."

"Red River Deli," Lula said. "It does a good lunch trade. It's in one of them gentrified high-crime areas."

Vinnie reappeared. He had his arms wrapped around a paper grocery bag, and he had a Red River Deli ball cap on his head.

"I got your uniforms here," Vinnie said to Lula and me. "Aprons and ball caps."

Lula leaned forward. "Say what?"

"Harry has decided he needs to diversify," Connie said. "He's not going to sell the deli. He's going to keep it and run it."

"I'm not seeing the connection," Lula said.

"Harry wants to keep the businesses under one umbrella," Vinnie said. "So, he's made Stephanie deli manager, and you're the assistant manager."

"I don't know anything about running a deli," I said. "And when am I supposed to do *this* job?"

"The deli doesn't open until noon," Vinnie said. "It's not like a grocery deli. It's more of a restaurant deli. You've got a couple line cooks and a waitress who do all the work. You just have to keep things running nice and smooth. You start today.

The keys are in the bag. Deli opens at noon, but the cooks come in at ten."

"No," I said. "I already have a job that I suck at. I don't need another one."

"Yeah," Lula said. "Me too."

"You'll get five hundred dollars a week plus lunch," Vinnie said to me.

I reached for the bag. "I'll take it."

"What about me?" Lula asked. "What do I get?"

"You get lunch," Vinnie said. "You already draw a salary for doing nothing."

"Works for me," Lula said. "I like lunch. It's one of my favorite things."

I'm five foot seven with blue eyes, shoulder-length curly brown hair, and a body that won't get me a job walking the Victoria's Secret runway but is good enough to get me a boyfriend. Lula is two inches shorter than me and has a lot more volume. Much of the volume is in boobs and booty, giving her a voluptuousness that would be hard to duplicate with surgery. Lula achieved her voluptuousness the old-fashioned way. Pork chops, fried chicken, biscuits and gravy, tubs of mac and cheese and potato salad, barbecue ribs, chili hot dogs. Her hair was magenta today. Her skin is polished mahogany. Her dress and five-inch stiletto heels are from her Saturday night 'ho collection and two sizes too small. The overall effect is spectacular, as usual.

I stuffed the new files into the deli bag, and Lula and I headed out.

"I think we should take *your* car," Lula said. "I just had my baby detailed, and that neighborhood is gentrified from what it used to be but that don't mean it's perfect."

Lula's baby is a shiny, perfectly maintained red Firebird with a sound system that could shake the fillings loose from your teeth. My car is an ancient faded blue Chevy Nova. It has a lot of rust, and a while back someone rudely spray-painted *pussy* on it. I covered the writing with silver Rust-Oleum glitter paint that was on sale. Unfortunately, I didn't have enough paint to cover the whole car.

I got into the Nova and pulled the Gurky file out of the bag.

"We don't have to be at the deli until ten," I said to Lula. "We have time to do a drive-by on Annie Gurky. According to her file she lives in an apartment complex in Hamilton Township. Married with two adult children. Age seventy-two."

"What did she shoplift?"

"A box of Tastykake Butterscotch Krimpets, a family-size bag of M&M's, a carton of Marlboros, two bags of Fritos, and a box of Twinkies. Apparently, she had them shoved into her tote bag and walked out of the store. An employee chased her across the parking lot, and she punched him in the nose."

"Did she drive away?" Lula asked.

"No. The police report says she couldn't remember where she parked her car. She was working her way through the box of Butterscotch Krimpets when she was arrested."

"Well, at least she's got good judgment when it comes to dessert. You can't do much better than Tastykakes and Twinkies."

# CHAPTER TWO

I MADE A U-turn in front of the bonds office and drove to Hamilton Township. Gurky lived around the corner from Delio's gas station. She was in a large, sprawling complex of two-story buildings that each housed six garden-level apartments and six second-floor apartments. Gurky was in a garden-level apartment. She answered the door with a smile. I introduced myself and explained to her that she'd missed her court date and would need to come with me to reschedule.

"I'm in the middle of breakfast," she said. "Maybe some other time."

Lula grinned. "Lady, you smell like you're having a hundred-proof breakfast."

"I like a splash of vodka in my orange juice," Gurky said.

"This won't take long," I told her. "We'll put the orange juice in the fridge, and you can finish it when you get back."

"This is all a misunderstanding," she said. "I wasn't stealing anything. I just forgot to pay. And then that horrible man attacked me."

"The one you punched in the nose?" Lula asked.

"Yes. That's the one. The purse snatcher. He tried to rob me. He grabbed my tote bag."

"You might have been confused on account of you had too much orange juice," Lula said.

"I need a lot of orange juice," Gurky said. "I have a lot of anger. I've been married to the same man for fifty-two years and last month he decided I wasn't 'doing it for him anymore,' so he ran off with my sister. My sister! I always knew she was a slut. And he took my cat, Miss Muffy. He never even *liked* Miss Muffy."

"Boy, that's so crummy," Lula said. "What a pig. You know what we should do? We should get Miss Muffy back. We should catnap her."

"We're not in the catnap business," I said to Lula. "And you're allergic to cats." I looked at my watch. Time was ticking away. We had to open the deli's doors for the cooks at ten o'clock. "We need to take you downtown to check in with the court," I said to Gurky. "We'll help you lock up the house."

"I won't have to stay in jail, will I?" Gurky asked.

"No," I told her. "Court is in session. We'll get you rescheduled and rebonded."

A half hour later we buckled Gurky into the back seat of my Nova. She'd put on lipstick, changed her shoes, slurped down some more orange juice, checked her door locks fifteen times, and tried to sneak out her back door.

"This is going to be tight," Lula said. "I don't see how you're going to drop her off at the courthouse and get back to the deli in time."

"I'll stop at the deli first, open the door and make sure everyone gets in, and then we'll take Gurky to the courthouse."

"Good thinking," Lula said. "That'll work."

Red River Deli isn't anywhere near a river. It's near the train station, next to a hotel that rents rooms by the hour. The gentrification process put in streetlamps that looked like gaslights, and brick-fronted a bunch of row houses and apartment buildings that previously had looked like a slum. The row houses and apartment buildings were gutted and renovated and sold to young professionals who worked in New York and wanted to be close to the train station. Unfortunately, some of the vagrants and gangbangers who roamed the area didn't get the gentrification memo so from time to time the area could be a little sketchy.

I parked on the street in front of the deli, and Lula and I looked over our shoulders at Annie Gurky in the back seat. Her hands were cuffed in front of her for comfort, and she was slumped over, softly snoring.

"Looks like she's sleeping off all that orange juice," Lula said. "Seems a shame to wake her. Maybe we should just crack a window and lock her in."

*"Hey!"* I said. *"Annie!"*

No response.

Two men were standing in front of the deli. One was Caucasian and the other looked Indian subcontinent. They were wearing baggy striped chef's pants, white chef's coats, and Red River Deli ball caps turned backward. They were smoking weed and texting.

"Guess those are our chefs," Lula said. "They look real professional. They got chef suits and everything. Maybe we should put our hats on."

"Maybe not," I said.

"Personally, I'm all about being an assistant restaurant manager," Lula said. "It's a excellent advancement opportunity. I hope you're not going to rain on my parade."

"There is no parade. We know *nothing* about running a restaurant. We have no experience."

"That's not true. I eat in restaurants all the time. And I saw *Ratatouille.*"

"*Ratatouille* is a cartoon."

"Well, I watch other shows too. I used to watch *Hell's Kitchen* with that cranky Ramsay guy."

I got out of the car and Lula followed. I introduced myself and asked the two men if they were our chefs.

"We are very much so," the smaller man said. "My name is Raymond. I have my green card."

The other chef was lanky and about six foot tall. He had black hair, a soul patch, and a gold tooth. He looked down at me through a weed haze.

"Stretch," he said.

"Even I do not know his true name," Raymond said. "He has always been Stretch."

I unlocked the front door and told them they couldn't smoke weed inside.

"This is not a good beginning," Raymond said. "I'm hoping you do not have more onerous rules we must follow."

Stretch playfully put his hand on Lula's boob, and Lula kicked him in the nuts. Stretch doubled over and sucked air.

"Onerous that rule," Lula said, and she sashayed inside.

The deli consisted of one room with booths lining two walls. Six tables for four were positioned in the middle of the room, and there was counter seating on the far end. The floors were scarred wood. The booths were red leather. Lighting was close to daylight and appropriate for a deli. There was a very slight lingering odor of fried onion rings, but overall it didn't smell bad. In fact, it smelled good if you were a fan of onion rings.

I walked past the counter seating and entered the kitchen. It was a galley setup with a large pantry to one side. It looked almost clean. I didn't see any roaches that were sneakers-up. I took that as a good sign.

I looked at a plastic-coated menu. Sandwiches, hot and cold. The usual sides. Standard deli desserts. Nothing complicated. Maybe Lula and I could pull this off.

"Okay," I said to Raymond and Stretch. "I'm sure you know what you're doing here. Lula and I will check back around noon."

"Whoa, not so fast," Stretch said. "What about the deliveries?"

"What about them?"

"You have to take inventory and schedule them. Then you have to make sure we get the right stuff on time. And you have to arrange for payment."

"You don't do that?"

"I make sandwiches, Cookie Puss."

I looked over at Raymond. "What about him?"

"He's the fry guy."

"Who did it yesterday?" I asked.

"No one," Stretch said. "So, we're up shit's creek today. We had a manager, but he disappeared. Went out for a break two days ago and never came back. He's the third manager in two weeks to disappear."

"And we always find one shoe," Raymond said. "One manager shoe by the dumpster, but no manager."

"Do the police know about this?"

"Oh yes," Raymond said. "They have been fully informed. They said it is a great mystery."

"I'm glad I'm not the new manager," Lula said to me. "I wouldn't want to be in his shoes . . . especially since sometime soon he could be left with only one. I would hate that. I take my shoes seriously."

"I'm the new manager," I said.

"Oh yeah," Lula said. "I forgot for a minute. Bummer. On the other hand, you could see the bright side and think this might be like *Cinderella*. She left a shoe behind and look how good it turned out for her."

"I can't take inventory right now," I told Stretch. "You're going to have to do it. Order whatever you need. I'll be back before you open at noon."

"I need a raise," Stretch said. "Can I order *that*?"

Lula and I walked out of the deli and stopped in the middle of the sidewalk.

"Where did we park the car?" Lula asked.

"Here," I said. "We parked it right here in front of the deli."

"I don't usually like to jump to conclusions, but I think someone stole your car," Lula said. "It might have been that Annie Gurky. She could have woke up and needed more orange juice."

That would be the best-case scenario. The worst would be that some thug took the car with Annie Gurky in it. I hauled my cellphone out of my bag and placed a call.

There are two men in my life. Joe Morelli is a Trenton cop who works plainclothes in crimes against persons. Morelli and I have a long history together that includes being engaged and not being engaged and several times almost being engaged. He has a nice little house on Slater Street that he inherited from his

Aunt Rose. He has a big orange dog, two brothers, two sisters, and a crazy grandmother named Bella. He's also totally sexy in an Italian movie star, homicide detective kind of way. The other guy is Ricardo Carlos Manoso, better known as Ranger. He's Latino. He's former Special Forces. He's hot. He owns Rangeman, a high-end security business operating out of a high-tech, low-profile building in downtown Trenton. And he's dedicated to keeping me alive and in sight. His motives aren't entirely altruistic.

"Are you calling the cops?" Lula asked.

"No. I'm calling Ranger. It's the fastest way to find my car."

# CHAPTER THREE

RANGER ATTACHES TRACKING devices to my cars. It was initially annoying, but I've gotten used to it, and in all honesty, it's come in handy on occasions like this.

"Babe," Ranger said.

Depending on the inflection, *Babe* could mean many things. Irritation, affection, desire, curiosity. Today it was without inflection. Today it was simply hello.

"My car is missing," I said. "I parked it in front of Red River Deli, and now it's gone."

There was silence while he pulled my car up on his computer.

"It's on lower Stark Street," Ranger said. "Probably headed for the chop shop on the fourth block. I'll send someone out to retrieve it."

"It might have an elderly woman in the back seat."

"Anyone I know?"

"Doubtful. I was returning her to the court."

"Babe," Ranger said. And he disconnected.

"Now what?" Lula asked.

"We wait," I said.

Ranger keeps several mobile units constantly patrolling accounts throughout the city. He was going to send one of them to Stark to intercept my car, and I was hoping he'd send another to rescue me.

Five minutes passed and a shiny black SUV rolled down the street and stopped at the curb. A guy who looked like a Marine recruit got out and motioned us into the back seat. He was wearing black Nikes, black cargo pants, and a form-fitting black T-shirt. The T-shirt had a Rangeman logo on the short sleeve that spanned his bulging biceps.

"Hal has your car," he said. "Did you know there's a woman in the back seat?"

"Yes. Is she okay?"

"Hal said she was asleep."

My car was parked one block off Stark. A black Rangeman SUV was parked behind it, and Hal was standing between the two cars. Hal is an over-muscled giant who faints at the sight of blood. A couple of skinny teens were sitting on the curb. Their hands were cuffed behind their backs, and one looked like he'd smashed his face into Hal's massive fist.

"Are you feeling all right?" I asked Hal.

"Yeah," Hal said. "He's only bleeding a little. It was an accident."

"I bet. What are you going to do with them?"

"Turn them loose. They're under the age limit." Hal grinned. "They freaked out when I told them they kidnapped an old lady. They hadn't noticed her in the back seat."

I glanced in at Annie. She was still sleeping.

I thanked Hal, and I called Connie to tell her we would be turning Annie Gurky over to the court in about fifteen minutes, and she would want to get rebonded. Lula and I weren't certified to write bond, so Connie or Vinnie would have to make a trip downtown.

Lula and I got into my Nova, and I drove to the police station. I pulled into the lot across from the municipal building, and Annie woke up.

"Are we here already?" she asked.

I walked her through the front door and left her with the desk lieutenant. I told him someone would be in shortly to bond her out so he shouldn't misplace her.

"We gotta get back to the deli," Lula said. "It's almost noon and I want my free lunch."

I wasn't anxious to get back to the deli. Truth is, I was thinking about bailing on the deal. I was freaked by the manager disappearances and the fact that my car had been stolen the instant I stepped away from it.

"I think I might quit," I told Lula. "Vinnie can find someone else to be manager."

"You can't quit," Lula said. "You've only just got the job. How do you know you don't like it? And we've never even had any of our free lunches. I already memorized the menu. I'm gonna have a number twelve and a number sixteen and a number twenty-two today."

"Three sandwiches?"

"Number twenty-two is a dessert."

I gave up a sigh, returned to my Nova, and headed for the deli. I would quit *after* lunch.

"I'm always excited about new beginnings," Lula said. "This could turn into something big for us. I got a good feeling about this."

"I have a *horrible* feeling about this. What about the disappearing managers?"

"It could be a big hoax. Like a joke. Or fake news. There's a lot of that fake news going around these days. Heck, we could be in the middle of a reality show. It's not like they found mutilated dead bodies. They just found a shoe, so how bad could it be?"

I cruised past the deli, looking for a parking place. There weren't any open spaces, so I drove down the one-lane alley that intersected the block and found parking next to the deli's small dumpster. Lula and I entered through the back door and tiptoed through the kitchen.

Raymond was working the fry station and griddle. Stretch was assembling sandwiches and plating. A twentysomething woman with a blond ponytail and a lot of tattoos was waiting tables. She was wearing jeans and a tank top and looked like she could kick my ass.

"Howdy," Lula said to her. "I'm Lula, the new assistant manager, and this is Stephanie Plum, standing next to me. She's the new manager."

"Dalia Koharchek," the woman said, extending her hand to me, looking down at my feet. "Congratulations, you've still got two shoes."

"About those managers . . . " I said.

"Number seven up," Stretch said.

Dalia grabbed two plates off the service counter and whisked them away to a booth.

"I want my lunch now," Lula said to Stretch. "A number twelve with extra bacon and a sixteen."

"Yeah, and I want a BJ," he said. "You know what our chances of getting any of those anytime soon are?"

"You should be more careful," Lula said. "That might be considered a sexually improper response."

Stretch sliced a hoagie roll and threw some shredded lettuce in it. "Bite me."

I grabbed Lula by the arm and dragged her out of the kitchen.

"He's lucky he said that to *me* on account of those off-color remarks don't bother me," Lula said. "I even kind of like them, but there's less-fun people who would report him to the PC police, and he could be in big trouble."

"Hey, Cookie Puss," Stretch yelled. "I got shorted by my purveyor. You're gonna need to do a market run."

"My name is Stephanie," I said. "*Stephanie.*"

"Yeah, whatever," Stretch said. "We got an account at the market two blocks down. I need six dozen eggs and four loaves of thick-cut white bread."

"I'll keep an eye open here," Lula said to me. "Since you're going shopping anyway, I'd appreciate it if you could pick up a *Star* magazine."

I walked the two blocks, bought my eggs, bread, and *Star* magazine, and walked back. Lula was standing on the sidewalk in front of the deli, and she was waving at me.

"I need a Xanax," Lula said. "I'm having hallucinations. I just saw a man disappear in a puff of smoke. He wasn't any ordinary man, either. He was like Satan, if Satan was totally hot and wearing black Armani. I could tell this wasn't even an Armani knockoff. Actually, it might not have been Armani. It might have been Tom Ford. I'm having a hormone attack. He looked me in the eye and I think I might have had an orgasm. Maybe it was just a rush. I was too flustered to appreciate it. Am I sweating? Is my face red? Maybe I don't need a Xanax. Maybe I just need a sandwich. I could be hallucinating from hunger."

"Where was this man?" I asked.

"He popped out of the little alleyway between the buildings. I came out here to get some air, and he just suddenly appeared."

"Did he say anything?"

"No," Lula said. "He just stood there, staring. It felt like my skin was on fire. And then he waved his hand, and there was a flash of light and a whoosh of smoke, and he was gone."

"Dark hair, dark eyes, slim?" I asked. "About six foot tall?"

"Yeah," Lula said. "And wicked hot. Do you know him?"

"Maybe. A while back I ran across a man who had a flair for the dramatic and fit that description."

"And he could disappear in smoke?" Lula asked.

"He's a magician. Among other things. His name is Gerwulf Grimoire. Most people know him as Wulf. He's Swiss born, and he speaks perfect English with a slight British accent."

"'Gerwulf Grimoire' is a horrible name," Lula said. "It could leave you damaged to have a name like that. You could be tainted."

I didn't think Wulf was tainted, but I didn't think he was normal, either. Wulf was a slightly scary enigma.

I gave Lula her magazine and handed the bread and eggs over to Stretch.

"We got a big takeout order," Stretch said. "It's on the counter behind me. Takeout boxes are on the overhead shelves."

"And?"

"And fill it. I'm going flat-out, and Raymond's up to his tits in fries."

I looked at the list on the counter. Ten sandwiches, four fries, six sides of slaw, two mac and cheese, one rice pudding, and two pieces of apple pie.

"Move over," Lula said. "I'm all about this." She took a red flowered scarf out of her purse and wrapped it around her hair bandanna style. "Where's my hat? I need my hat."

I gave her one of the hats and took a step back.

"You get to be the sous chef," Lula said, taking the list from me. "Put your hat on and get me a loaf of bread. It says here we gotta start with a number seven. What the heck is a number seven?"

"I thought you had the menu memorized."

"I only memorized the ones I wanted to eat. Some fool don't know better than to order a number seven. Maybe we should do him a favor and give him a number twelve."

"The menu says a number seven is turkey and Swiss on whole grain."

"Three ounces of turkey and two slices of Swiss," Stretch said. "The turkey is pre-measured. Mustard on the Swiss side and mayo on the turkey. Every sandwich gets two deli pickles."

"Boy, they got this to a science," Lula said. "Everything's in these bins. All I need is the bread. Who eats multigrain, anyway? Multigrain don't melt in your mouth like white bread."

I gave Lula the bread and she slathered mustard on one and mayo on the other. She added the turkey and Swiss and shook her head.

"This isn't a Lula sandwich," she said. "I can't be proud sending out a sandwich like this." She added Tabasco and two strips of bacon. "This person is gonna thank me. I'm giving them a superior culinary experience."

She sliced the sandwich in half, and I put it in one of the plastic containers with two pickles.

"You gotta move faster," Stretch said. "Pickup's waiting."

"You gotta chill," Lula said. "I'm making gastrointestinal history. You can't rush this artistic shit."

We slapped together nine more sandwiches, got the sides put together and boxed up the pie. Dalia bagged everything and took it all to the pickup counter.

"I need pie," Lula said. "I got a pie craving."

"What about the sandwiches you wanted?"

"I ate a lot of the fixings while we were doing the takeout order, but I didn't get any pie."

Connie called on my cellphone. "I'm at the courthouse, and there's no Annie Gurky. Did you get a receipt for her?"

"No," I said. "I was in a rush to get back to the deli, so I told the cop at the desk to give you the receipt."

"He's saying you didn't make it clear that she needed to be held."

"She was cuffed!"

"He might not have noticed. Anyway, responsibility is in a gray zone right now, so see if you can find her. She probably called Uber and is back in her house."

I looked out at the dining area. The lunch trade seemed to be winding down. Half of the booths were empty.

"I'm taking off for a while," I said to Stretch. "Things to do." Like tell Vinnie he should hire a new manager.

"You need to be back here at five o'clock," Stretch said. "It gets nuts when the rush hour trains roll in."

"And do not go out the back door," Raymond said.

"My car is parked in the back," I said.

"No, no, no," he said. "Do not ever park there. We call that the Domain of the Death Dumpster. That is where managers go to disappear."

"I'll keep that in mind," I said, "but I'm going to chance it this one time."

Raymond handed me a meat cleaver. "Take this with you. You must protect yourself."

"She don't need that," Lula said. "I'm packing a loaded Glock. And I'm taking a pie as backup."

"Good luck," Raymond said. "Keep your eyes open. I hope you return. We will soil ourselves trying to get through the evening covers without an extra hand."

Lula pulled a pumpkin pie from the fridge, grabbed a fork, and followed me out. She stopped in the middle of the small lot and looked around.

"So, this is where it happens," she said. "I guess it's like *poof* and no more manager. Just a shoe left behind. Maybe it's aliens beaming up managers. That would be the most logical explanation. I could see that happening."

"Why would aliens leave a shoe behind?"

"It could be a thoughtful gesture so his family knew he was taken by aliens. Or maybe when you get beamed up your shoe falls off. It could be a side effect of beaming up. If you don't mind I'm not standing too close to you in case you suddenly get beamed up."

I allowed myself a grimace and a single eye roll, and I got into my Nova. Lula buckled up next to me and forked into the pie.

"Annie Gurky wandered away from the police station," I said to Lula. "Connie is canvassing the area around the municipal building, and I'm going to go back to Annie's house."

"It would be bad if someone finds one of her shoes," Lula said. "That would mean the aliens were looking to diversify in their beaming."

# CHAPTER FOUR

LULA WAS HALFWAY through the pie when I pulled into Annie's apartment complex. I parked in one of the guest spaces allotted to her unit, left Lula in the car, and went to Annie's door. I rang the bell three times. No answer. I looked in her front windows. No sign that she was inside. Her car was parked in the lot. I went back to my car and called Annie's cellphone.

She answered on the second ring.

"Hey," I said. "Where are you?"

"Who is this?"

"It's Stephanie Plum."

"Well, then, I'm at the police station."

"I know you aren't at the police station. I hear noise in the background. Omigod, are you at the airport?"

"Of course not."

"You are. I just heard them announce a flight to Miami."

Annie disconnected.

I banged my head against the steering wheel and told Lula that Annie was at the airport.

"She's sneaky," Lula said. "You gotta respect that."

"I'm going back to the office," I said. "I want to talk to Vinnie."

"You aren't going to quit the deli job, are you? That would be a big mistake. *Huge* mistake. We got a future with sandwiches. I could see people traveling for hours just to get one of our sandwiches. We could be up there with the Amazon guy and the Facebook guy except with sandwiches. I'm thinking about taking out patents on my sandwich creations. You know that last sandwich that we made where we started to run out of stuff so we put in whatever was left?"

"The sandwich with the green sliced turkey?"

"Yeah. I'm thinking about getting a patent on that one and calling it the Garbage Truck."

I thought it might be more accurately called the Salmonella Special.

I left the apartment complex, drove to the office, and parked.

"The place looks closed up," Lula said.

We got out and went to the door. Locked. No lights on inside. I called Connie.

"Where are you?" I asked her.

"I'm still at the courthouse. Did you find Annie Gurky?"

"No. I'm at the office and it's locked. Where's Vinnie?"

"I don't know, and I don't want to know. Try his cellphone."

I called Vinnie's cellphone and home phone. No answer on either.

"This is fate stepping in," Lula said. "Fate doesn't want you to quit the deli."

I was standing in the middle of the sidewalk, thinking fate was a load of baloney, when Morelli cruised down the street. He hooked an illegal U-turn and pulled in behind my car.

It was September and Jersey was still feeling like summer. Morelli was wearing jeans and a button-down shirt with the sleeves rolled. His hair was curling over his ears and down the back of his neck, and he had a five o'clock shadow a couple hours early. He smiled at me, and my doodah got happy.

"I was just about to call you," he said. "Are you up for burgers tonight?"

Morelli and I don't live together, but I keep a change of clothes and a toothbrush at his house. Burgers would be good. What followed would be even better.

"Burgers sound okay, but I might be late," I said. "I'm helping out at the Red River Deli."

"Yeah, she's the new manager," Lula said. "And I'm the assistant manager."

Morelli wrapped his hand around my arm and pulled me to the side of the building.

"I suppose you want to have a private conversation," Lula yelled after us. "I'll just wait in the car, being that I'm tired from eating all that pie anyways."

"Are you serious?" Morelli asked me. "Manager?"

"The agency was awarded the deli on a bond foreclosure. Harry's decided to keep it, and he asked me to be manager."

"Do you know why he's decided to keep it?" Morelli asked. "It's because no one will buy it. It's known as the Demon Deli. Sometimes it's called the Death Deli. And on special occasions it's the Deli of Doom or the One-Shoe Horror."

"I hadn't heard it called any of those names."

"Do you know about the managers? Three managers have disappeared in two weeks. Always leaving a shoe behind. No other clue. Not a shred of evidence. They just went through the back door and evaporated."

"Is it your case?"

"Jimmy Krut pulled it but I'm the secondary. I came in when the third manager disappeared."

"I didn't know about the disappearances when I took the job this morning. I found out when I got to the deli."

"It hasn't received a lot of publicity. The first manager who disappeared had been manager for six years. Elroy Ruiz. Entire family was in Mexico. He sent most of his money home. He went out to smoke some weed at eight-fifteen on a Monday night and never came back. They said it wasn't the first time Elroy took off for a while. No one thought anything about it until Wednesday. Didn't get reported to the police until Friday."

"What about the shoe? Didn't they think it was odd that his shoe was left in the parking lot?"

Morelli grinned. "Everyone thought he was on a good buzz."

"And the second manager?"

"Kenny Brown. Twenty-six years old. Ten years of restaurant experience. Started washing dishes when he was sixteen. Lived with his mother. Straight arrow except for his coke habit."

"The drug?"

"The drink. Was on the job for a week. Took a bag of garbage out to the dumpster around nine o'clock and never came back. Everyone assumed he'd left for the night. One of the cooks found Brown's car still parked in the lot the next day. Brown's shoe was next to it. The third manager, Ryan Meier, lasted two days. The little fry cook freaked when he went out to look for the manager and tripped over the shoe in the dark."

"Is this happening anyplace else?"

"No. Just at Red River Deli. And just to managers . . . so far."

"Jeez."

"Yup," Morelli said. "That about sums it up. Tell me you're not going back there."

"I was going to quit but Vinnie isn't in the office."

"Send him a text message."

I typed the message into my phone. *As of this instant I quit my job as manager of Red River Deli.*

"I'll throw the burgers on the grill at six o'clock," Morelli said.

I returned to my car and buckled myself in.

"Did you see him?" Lula asked. "It was the hot guy in black. Wulf. He was in a shiny black 4×4 pickup with oversized tires and bug eyes on the cab. He drove right past us and turned at the corner."

"I wasn't paying attention to the traffic," I said. "I was talking to Morelli."

"How'd that go?" Lula asked.

"Good. He's grilling burgers tonight, and I texted Vinnie that I quit."

"I've been thinking about it, and maybe this is a good thing. Maybe Vinnie will make *me* manager. It could get me a raise."

"You aren't afraid you'll disappear?"

"I have it figured out. I won't go near the parking lot. I'll always go out the front door."

"What about the garbage?"

"I'll send it out with Stretch. He doesn't have to worry on account of he's a cook. And I'll be the manager, so I can assign him garbage detail. Only problem is we have to find Vinnie, so we can make the job switch. Of course, you quit in a text message, so I guess I could text him that I'm taking over as manager."

I slipped Wayne Kulicki's file out of my bag. "I need to find this guy."

"If you're hard up for money now that you're not a manager, I might hire you as a waitress or dishwasher or something."

"I'll keep that in mind. Are you coming with me or are you going back to the deli?"

"I'll ride with you so long as I get back to the deli by five o'clock."

Wayne Kulicki was renting a small one-bedroom row house

on the fringe of Chambersburg. He'd been a trust officer with a local bank prior to going bonkers and destroying the Eat and Go. He was currently unemployed.

I drove one block down Hamilton Avenue, turned into the Burg, and wound around the maze of streets that led to the row houses. Kulicki's house was third from the corner and not in great shape. The paint was peeling off the clapboard, and one of his two front windows was cracked.

I parked in front of the house, and Connie called.

"Where are you?" Connie asked.

"I'm in front of Wayne Kulicki's house. Where are you?"

"I'm in the parking lot behind the office. Vinnie's car is here. And his shoe."

"Is Vinnie's foot in the shoe?"

"No."

"Is Vinnie in the office?"

"No."

"You're kidding, right?"

"No, I'm not kidding," Connie said. "I called his cell, and there's no answer. I called his wife, and she hasn't seen him since this morning."

"Is there any sign of struggle? Blood?"

"No. None of that. Just the shoe."

"This is too bizarre. Are you sure Vinnie isn't hanging out somewhere watching you, laughing his ass off?"

"I don't hear any laughing," Connie said. "Do you think I should call the police? It's not like I could definitely say I'm looking at a crime scene. And suppose I'm being punked, and I'm too stupid to know it?"

"Do you know Jimmy Krut?"

"Yes. I went to school with him," Connie said.

"Give him a call. He's the primary on the deli disappearances."

I disconnected and told Lula about the shoe.

"That's not fitting the profile," Lula said. "That's changing the modus operandi. Someone's got a lot of nerve doing that. I was counting on being able to go out the front door. And Vinnie isn't even the deli manager. Of course, he's the bonds office manager so maybe that's got a relationship there."

"Do you still want to be manager of the deli?"

"Hell no. Those space aliens got a manager fixation."

I was having a hard time believing that Vinnie had gotten beamed up, chopped up, or otherwise abducted. It was too weird. I needed more proof than a shoe. I needed a video, a bloody handprint, a text message. I needed something confirming that a disaster had occurred. I mean, anybody could lose a shoe, right? And how do we know it wasn't planted by Vinnie so he could go off and get spanked by Madam Zaretsky?

"So, what are we going to do now?" Lula asked.

"We're going to see if Wayne Kulicki is home."

I knocked on his door, and he answered on the second knock.

"What?" he said.

He was fifty-six years old, five foot ten, balding, and soft around the middle. He was wearing a stained T-shirt and boxer shorts, and he was holding a gun.

"Whoa," Lula said. "That's no way to answer a door. Where's your manners? You don't say 'What?' in that tone. You say 'Hello' and you smile on account of there's two ladies on your doorstep. And besides, what's with the gun?"

"I'm thinking of killing myself."

"If I was you I'd change my shirt first. You don't want to clock out with a stained T-shirt," Lula said.

"I represent Vincent Plum Bail Bonds," I said to Kulicki. "You missed your court date and need to come with us to reschedule."

"I can't go now. I have an important decision to make."

"Maybe we can help you," Lula said. "What are you thinking about?"

"Killing myself."

"There's lots of decisions associated with that," Lula said. "I assume you're gonna shoot yourself in the head."

"Yeah," Kulicki said.

"Well, your head will most likely explode and make a big mess when you shoot yourself, so best to do it in the bathroom or kitchen. And then are you going to leave a note? And you'll probably poop your pants so you gotta decide if boxers are the best choice or do you want to be wearing something more sturdy?"

"Mostly I was just thinking if I *should* do it," Kulicki said.

"I'd advise against it," Lula said. "It's not something you can change your mind on after you do it. And suppose the bullet doesn't go in exactly right and you turn yourself into an unsightly vegetable?"

Kulicki nodded. "That's a concern."

"You bet your ass," Lula said. "Why do you want to kill yourself?"

"To begin with, I'm going to jail."

"It might not be so bad," Lula said. "I know lots of people in jail, and they're doing okay. Besides, you could get off with community service or something. You don't know for sure if you'll get jail time."

"Even if I don't go to jail my life is ruined. All because of some stupid fries."

"You got shorted at the drive-thru window, right?" Lula said.

"Yes. So, I went inside and asked for the manager."

"And there was no manager, right?" Lula said.

"Right! And then some green-haired imbecile with a nose ring who was behind the counter told me I was fat and didn't need more fries."

"I had that same thing happen to me," Lula said. "I hate that place."

"So, I was still polite," Kulicki said. "I told him he was rude and his comments were unprofessional and inappropriate."

"You exhibited excellent self-control," Lula said. "I told him he smelled like cucumber and cat pee, and I went around back where all the employees park and I keyed all their cars."

"I never thought of that."

"What happened next?" Lula asked.

"He gave me the finger and squirted mustard at me. It got all over my shirt and tie. And I guess I snapped. It was like I turned into the Hulk."

"It says on your report that you destroyed personal property and then set fire to it."

"The fire was an accident. One of the counter people tried to throw a pot of water at me but spilled it into the fryer by mistake, and *WHOOSH* next thing the whole kitchen was on fire."

"In my book, you're a hero," Lula said.

"You're the only one who thinks like that," Kulicki said. "My wife is divorcing me. She got a restraining order against me and kicked me out of my house. My kids won't talk to me. And I got fired, and no one else will hire me. So that's why I'm thinking about killing myself."

Lula nodded. "Those are all good reasons."

"No, they *aren't* good reasons," I said. "I'm sure your kids will eventually understand. And maybe you'll be better off without your wife. She's not exactly supportive."

"Yeah," Lula said. "Do you have a good lawyer?"

"I can't afford a lawyer," he said. "I don't have a job."

"What kind of job are you looking for?"

"Any kind of job," Kulicki said.

"Have you ever heard of the Red River Deli?" Lula asked him.

"No," Kulicki said.

"Well, then, I have a good job for you," Lula said. "How would you like to be manager of the Red River Deli?"

"I don't know anything about running a deli."

"Don't matter," Lula said. "We're in charge of hiring, and we'd be willing to give you a shot at it." She looked over at me. "Right?"

"We're supposed to be returning him to the court," I said to Lula.

"Yeah, but we could do that tomorrow," Lula said. "I bet if we got this nice man a good job he'd be willing to turn himself in and get rebonded. And if he had a good job he probably wouldn't even want to kill himself."

"How much does it pay?" he asked.

"Five hundred a week on salary plus you get lunch," Lula said.

"I guess I could try out the manager job," he said. "It might be interesting after all those years at the bank."

"You'd be working with some real colorful characters," Lula said. "If you put some clothes on we could start you off right now."

# CHAPTER FIVE

IT WAS A couple minutes before five when we rolled up to the deli. People were trickling out of the train station, and there was more than the usual amount of traffic on the street. I circled the block three times before finding a place to park.

Kulicki was dressed in gray slacks and a blue button-down shirt with a small RGC logo embroidered on it. The shirt and slacks were slightly wrinkled, and I thought they were probably the clothes he'd had on when he got fired and locked out of his house.

Half the booths were filled when we walked into the deli, and there were two people standing at the takeout counter.

Raymond looked up from his fry station when we brought Kulicki into the kitchen. Stretch went hands on hips.

"Who's this?" Stretch asked.

"This is Wayne Kulicki," Lula said. "He's the new manager. We're delegating authority."

"He have any experience?" Stretch asked.

"He's got a lot of experience," Lula said. "Just not in the deli industry."

Stretch shook his head and went back to chopping an onion.

"All you gotta do is keep things running smooth," Lula said to Kulicki. "Sometimes you gotta make an emergency run to the grocery store down the street. And you gotta keep track of the food these guys need and make sure they don't run out."

"Sure," Kulicki said. "I can do that."

"Does he know about the shoe?" Stretch asked.

"He knows he's gotta wear them," Lula said. "We don't want managers without shoes."

"No," I said. "He doesn't know about the shoe."

"It would be a bad thing to give him this job and not tell him about the shoe," Raymond said. "It would put your karma in the shitter."

"The last three managers have mysteriously disappeared," I said to Kulicki. "No one knows what happened to them. They went out the back door and never returned."

"And always there was one of their shoes left by the dumpster," Raymond said. "It is the best part of the story."

"What do you think happened to them?" Kulicki asked.

"I'm pretty sure it was space aliens," Lula said. "It's something they would do."

"Order up," Stretch yelled.

Dalia swooped in, whisked two plates off the service counter, and took them to a booth. Two more people joined the takeout line. Dalia took their orders and handed them over to Stretch. Stretch passed them over to me, and I gave them to Kulicki.

"You're the takeout order filler," I said to Kulicki.

"And I'm going to work with you," Lula said. "I'm the celebrity sandwich maker." She looked around. "Where are the hats? We need our hats."

"We can't all fit in the kitchen," I said. "I'm leaving, but I'll be back to close up and drive everyone home." I turned to Kulicki. "And then I'll pick you up tomorrow morning at nine o'clock and get you rebonded."

Morelli lives two minutes outside of the Burg and five minutes from the bonds office. His house is very similar to my parents' house. The front door opens to a tiny foyer that leads to the living room, the living room leads to the dining room, and the dining room leads to the kitchen. There are three small bedrooms upstairs plus a bathroom. Morelli has added a downstairs powder room and swapped out his aunt's dining room table for a billiard table.

I let myself in and braced for impact. I could hear Bob galloping through the house to greet me. He's a big sweetie pie, a floppy-eared dog with shaggy orange hair. He has no manners, and more enthusiasm than brains. He launched himself through the air when he saw me and body-slammed me back against the front door.

"Good dog!" I said.

I ruffled his ears and gave him a hug, and he trotted off, satisfied that he'd given me a proper welcome.

Morelli was in the kitchen. He had a beer in one hand and a spatula in the other. "Just in time," he said, wrapping an arm around me, giving me a kiss. "I was worried you might not show, and I'd have to eat all these burgers by myself."

"I left Lula at the deli. I said I would be back to close and drive her home."

"I heard about Vinnie and the shoe."

"It's weird, right?"

Morelli tossed a package of hamburger buns on a tray with the burgers and slices of cheese, and carried it all outside. "Yeah, it's weird. Hard to believe anyone would want to abduct Vinnie."

"Lula thinks it's space aliens."

"What do you think?" Morelli asked.

"I think it might be Ernie Sitz. Or someone associated with him."

Morelli put the burgers on the grill. "What about motive?"

"Maybe he's angry that he lost the deli and wants to get some sort of revenge."

"I'm having a hard time with revenge. Sitz isn't stupid. He had to know he was going to lose the deli when he used it as collateral against his bond. It was a calculated move. He traded the deli for his freedom. He never intended to hang around for his court appearance. He was out of the country less than twenty-four hours after Vinnie had him released."

"That leaves us with the space aliens theory."

Morelli grinned. "I like it. Takes the pressure off my department. Trenton PD doesn't get involved in intergalactic crime."

We ate burgers and chips and had ice cream for dessert. We walked Bob around the block and returned to the kitchen to do cleanup.

"Here's the deal," Morelli said, stuffing plates and utensils in the dishwasher. "The game doesn't start until eight tonight, so we have some time to kill."

"And?"

"I've missed you," he said.

He pulled me close and kissed me. His hands were warm at my waist and the kiss was soft. I felt a rush of desire swirl through my stomach and head south.

Morelli was like the post office. He always delivered. If the delivery vehicle ran out of gas, there was no need to panic. Morelli had battery backup.

"Maybe we should move this upstairs," Morelli said. "By the time I'm done we're going to need a shower."

Okay, this worked for me. We've had passionate experiences on the little kitchen table, bent over the kitchen counter, on the couch, the billiard table, the coffee table, the washing machine, and halfway up the stairs. His nice, big king-sized bed was definitely my favorite. I'll take comfort over novelty any day of the week. An orgasm is an orgasm, but getting there can leave you with a herniated disc if you aren't careful.

After the shower, we settled in to watch the game on Morelli's big-screen TV. It's a cozy seating arrangement since Morelli and I have to scrunch ourselves together at one end of the couch so Bob can sprawl at the other. My phone rang at nine-thirty.

"You gotta get here," Lula said. "I'm totally freaked. I need tranqs or a burrito or something."

"You're in a deli," I said. "Make yourself a grilled cheese."

"That's not going to do it. Maybe mac and cheese. I need a gallon of mac and cheese."

"There's a problem?" I asked Lula.

"Fuckin' A there's a problem. We got a freakin' shoe in the parking lot. Next to the dumpster."

"Oh boy."

"Exactly," Lula said. "It's a 'oh boy' problem."

"Do you know who belongs to the shoe?"

"Hell yeah. It's Kulicki's shoe. He was being all smart-ass about how nothing was going to happen to him. And how there weren't aliens beaming people up to their spaceship. And next thing he was taking a bag of garbage to the dumpster and *whoosh* no more Kulicki. Only his shoe."

"Did anyone see this happen?"

"No. We were all busy cleaning up and taking care of the last two customers. I couldn't even say how long he was gone. Stretch went to the storeroom and noticed the back door to the deli was open and the light was on in the parking area. He looked out and saw the shoe."

"Maybe Kulicki is playing a joke."

"We called out to him but he didn't answer," Lula said. "And Raymond and Stretch went outside, looking around, but they couldn't find him."

"Did you call the police?"

"I'm thinking that's what I'm doing now. And remember I need a ride to my car. It's at the office."

"Okeydokey then. I'll see you in a little bit."

I disconnected, gave up a sigh, and stood. "It looks like Kulicki lost a shoe."

"Who's Kulicki?"

"He was the new deli manager. We sort of hired him."

"And he lasted how long?"

I checked my watch. "Approximately four hours."

"Damn," Morelli said. "Those aliens are good. They spotted a new manager after only four hours."

"You're thinking someone on the inside is involved."

"It's possible."

"There were only three people who knew Kulicki was the manager."

"Krut probably wants to talk to them . . . again."

I grabbed my messenger bag off the coffee table and hiked it onto my shoulder. "I have to roll."

"I'll roll with you. I want to make sure you don't get beamed up by mistake."

Morelli called Jimmy Krut from the car, and by the time we got to the deli there were already two uniforms on the scene. Krut arrived a couple minutes after us. Lula, Stretch, Raymond, and Dalia were hunkered down inside.

"This is getting very old," Raymond said to me. "I am thinking this is not such a good place to work." He looked over at Morelli. "I have a green card."

"Good for you," Morelli said. "Can I see it?"

"No," Raymond said. "It would not be possible to show it to you at this time. I fear I have misplaced it."

"You should try to find it," Lula said. "You could lose your job here without that green card."

"Fortunately, this is a sanctuary deli," Raymond said. "It is a prime consideration for maintaining employment at this establishment."

One of the uniforms ran a strip of crime scene tape across the back of the deli parking lot, and a photographer showed up to take pictures of the shoe before Krut bagged and labeled it. Morelli walked the alley with a flashlight, and I stayed inside and helped myself to a piece of coconut cream pie.

"We should get Vinnie to put up a security camera over the back door," Lula said. "Then we'd see next time someone got snatched."

"Vinnie is MIA," I said. "He's not going to be a lot of help here."

"I forgot," Lula said. "There's so many people missing I could hardly keep track of them."

I ate my pie and considered Raymond, Stretch, and Dalia. Morelli brought up a good point. Kulicki disappeared in record time. Not many people knew he was the manager. That information had to have been passed on from Raymond, Stretch, or Dalia.

We were all sitting in the dining area. Lula was checking out Facebook. Dalia was filing her nails. Raymond and Stretch were texting on their smartphones.

"Did any of you tell anyone we had a new manager?" I asked.

Everyone shook their head no.

"*Someone* knew," I said.

"Those space aliens got ways," Lula said. "They can probably read minds."

"How long must we sit here?" Raymond asked. "I have many things to do."

I went outside and found Krut. "How's it going?" I asked him.

"It's not," he said. "Nada. Bupkus. Nothing happening. How am I supposed to explain this to my wife? I got called out at ten o'clock at night because someone found a shoe by a dumpster. You know what she thinks? She thinks I've got something going on the side."

"Do you?"

"Not tonight," Krut said.

I looked back at the deli. "The natives are getting restless in there."

"Tell them they can go. If we need to talk to them we know where to find them."

I dismissed the troops and drove Lula to the office so she could get her car. I returned to the deli and tagged after Morelli.

He was done walking the alley, and he was examining the parking area around the dumpster.

"You really like this," I said.

He nodded. "I like police work in general, but this case is especially interesting. I'm sucked in by the single shoe left behind. It's a calling card."

"Someone is sending a message."

"Yeah. Too bad I don't know the content of the message. I only know the signature."

"What do you think has happened to all these people? Dead?"

"That's one possibility."

"What would be another?"

"I don't have another," Morelli said. "I suppose they could all be working at a bodega in Bogotá."

This was especially chilling since one of the victims was a man I'd deliberately put in harm's way and another was my cousin. I wasn't fond of Vinnie, but he was my cousin all the same.

"I'm not feeling good about this," I said.

"I'm not feeling good about you even being involved. There's a serious lunatic at work here, and so far, forensics isn't finding anything useful." He narrowed his eyes ever so slightly and looked at me. "You *aren't* involved, right?"

"Technically I might still be the manager."

"I thought you were going to quit."

"I sent Vinnie the text message when I was with you, but I

never got an answer. I suppose he was already beamed up or rubbed out or shipped off to Bogotá."

"My understanding is that the deli is owned by Harry. You can tell Harry you're no longer manager."

"You're right. I'll get in touch with Harry first thing in the morning."

# CHAPTER SIX

FIRST THING IN the morning for Morelli is different than first thing in the morning for me. Morelli is showered and dressed and out the door at the crack of dawn. I usually drag myself out of bed a couple hours later. This morning I heard him leave, and I lay in bed with my eyes wide open. I was plagued with guilt over Kulicki and concern for Vinnie. I always thought if Vinnie would just disappear it would be like my family was finally free of something horrible—like boils or ringworm or chronic bloat. Now that he really had disappeared, I found that my emotion wasn't the joy I'd expected. If I could put my finger on an emotion it would be grief. I was truly worried. Go figure.

I gave up on sleep and got dressed. I grabbed a waffle out of the freezer, hugged Bob, and drove back to my apartment while I gnawed on the waffle.

I live in a dated, uninspired, three-story building that straddles the Trenton city limits. I have one bedroom, one bathroom, one television, a kitchen, a dining alcove, and a living room. My furniture is mostly secondhand. My fridge contains beer, wine, Velveeta cheese slices, strawberry preserves, sometimes milk, olives, bread and butter pickles, various condiments, and on occasion leftover pizza.

I share the apartment with a hamster named Rex. He lives in an aquarium on my kitchen counter. He doesn't bark and he has very small poop, so he would be the perfect pet if I could just walk him on a leash.

I said hello to Rex and apologized for spending the night with Morelli. I gave him fresh water and food and told him I loved him. He blinked his round black eyes at me and twitched his whiskers.

"I have a problem," I said to Rex. "I agreed to take this very dangerous job. I didn't know it was dangerous when I took it. I found out when I showed up for work. So, I chickened out of the job and encouraged someone to take my place. It was someone who was in a vulnerable spot and thought I was doing him a favor. And now he's missing. And I feel sick inside."

I dropped a peanut into the cage, and Rex stuffed it into his cheek. He looked as if he still liked me even though I wasn't such a nice person for possibly getting Wayne Kulicki killed.

That's the good thing about having a hamster as a roommate. They're not judgmental as long as you give them an occasional peanut.

"And that's not all," I told Rex. "Vinnie is missing. We both know he's never been my favorite person, but as it turns out, I don't feel good about something bad happening to him. The police are involved, but I don't see them making much progress. I feel like I should be doing something to help. I'm a recovery agent. I'm supposed to be good at finding people."

Rex looked doubtful at this.

"True, I'm not the world's best recovery agent," I said, "but sometimes I get lucky."

I left Rex to enjoy his peanut, and I marched off to take a shower and change into clean clothes. Morelli wasn't going to be happy, but I had to do the right thing. I was going back to the deli. I was going to try to find Kulicki and Vinnie, dead or alive. And I was going to be careful not to end up snatched, leaving a single shoe behind.

A half hour later I returned to the kitchen, took my S&W .38 out of the brown bear cookie jar, and dropped it into my messenger bag. It probably wouldn't be effective against aliens from outer space, but it might be helpful against any psycho who wanted to ship me off to Bogotá.

I called Ranger and told him about my moral dilemma.

"Babe," Ranger said. "Your intentions are admirable, but chances are good that you'll die."

"I'd prefer not to die. I was hoping you could help me by

installing and manning some security cameras behind the deli."

"No problem." And he disconnected.

Ranger is a man of few words but lots of action.

Lula and Connie were already at the office when I rolled in.

"Any word from Vinnie?" I asked Connie.

She shook her head. "No. He hasn't been home. No one's seen him."

"I feel real sad," Lula said. "And I don't even like him."

"He could be okay," I said. "The aliens could bring him back."

"That's true," Lula said. "Sometimes people get returned after they've been probed. Ordinarily getting probed would be a traumatic experience, but Vinnie might like it. He could even come back in a good mood."

"I have some time before I have to open the deli," I said. "I'm going after Victor Waggle."

"You sure you want to be manager again?" Lula asked.

"Yes," I said. "I'm sure."

"You must be in a serious frame of mind," Lula said when we were in my car, pulling away from the curb. "You didn't even take a donut out of the box on Connie's desk. And that's too bad since it might be your last donut before losing your shoe."

"I'm not going to lose my shoe."

"You carrying?"

"Yes."

"Your gun got bullets in it?"

"No. I have to buy bullets."

"That's just pathetic that you haven't got bullets. You're gonna give the rest of us women a bad reputation. You can't even protect yourself, much less stop a terror attack. Good thing you got me along."

"Because you could stop a terror attack?"

"Hell, yeah. I'm ready to take them idiot terrorists down."

Hard to believe since Lula was the worst shot ever. She was known to miss a target at point-blank range.

"Jersey is full of those idiots," Lula said. "And we even got out-of-state idiots coming here. We got terrorists coming here from Connecticut and New York. You don't hear much about it because we got excellent law enforcement and they thwart the attacks."

"I suppose that's comforting."

"Yeah, but you don't want to get too comfortable because those terrorists might be idiots but they're sneaky idiots. It's only a matter of time before one of them slips in and rampages Jersey."

I knew I was going to regret asking, but I couldn't help myself. "Why Jersey?"

"All us good citizens in Jersey got attitude. We got pride. We got brass balls the size of watermelons. We got rude hand gestures and loaded guns . . . most of us. It's not like we're a pushover state like California. If you want to make points and get extra virgins when you blow yourself up, clearly

Jersey is the place to accomplish that, you see what I'm saying? It's not like we're easy."

I sucked in a grimace. It was always frightening when Lula made sense saying something stupid.

"And now that I'm thinking about it, that's probably the same reason the aliens chose a deli in Trenton to suck people up into their spaceship," Lula said. "Us Trentonians are a challenge. And for the most part we got good taste in shoes."

I handed the Waggle file to Lula. "I glanced at this briefly when Connie first gave it to me. I think he lives on Stark Street."

Lula thumbed through the file. "Yeah, but he's way at the end, just before the junkyard. You want to get bullets for your gun before you go there."

I cut across the downtown business district and turned right onto Stark.

"Drop me off at the beauty salon on the next block," Lula said. "I'll run in and get you some ammo."

"At the beauty salon?"

"Lateesha sells some merchandise on the side. She's been around for a long time. I used to shop there when I was a 'ho on account of my corner was only one block away. She's got a real good nail tech too."

I double-parked in front of the salon. Lula ran in and came out five minutes later.

"I got your stuff," Lula said. "And I got a kick-ass nail varnish. It's midnight blue with silver sparkles. I'm going to look like the night sky. I'm going to be like the Beatles song. Lula in the sky with diamonds."

Stark Street starts out okay with a couple blocks of legitimate businesses. The third block begins to get dicey, and it goes downhill fast from there. By the time you get to the burned-out, gutted buildings at the end of Stark the only residents are rats and loonies. A very prosperous junkyard sits about a mile beyond the last building.

We were one block from the end, idling in front of a two-story brick building that looked like it used to be a warehouse. It was the only structure still standing. Everything else on the block was rubble.

"This has to be the block," Lula said. "Hard to believe he's living here. And if he is living here, I'm not going in to root him out. The police won't even come to this block. There's gonna be rats and snakes and unfortunate people's body parts in this building we're looking at."

"Body parts?" I asked.

"I'm just supposing."

I made a U-turn and slowly drove back down Stark, hoping for a Waggle sighting. "What else do we have? Workplace? Relatives? Girlfriend?"

"He's self-employed," Lula said, reading through the file. "He gives that building back there as his home and place of business. Looks like his family is all in Wisconsin."

"Who posted Waggle's bond?"

"A guy named Leonard Skoogie. It was a high bond, and it looks like it was secured with cash."

"Do we have an address for Skoogie?"

"Suite twelve in the Hamilton Building on State Street."

I was familiar with the Hamilton Building. It was one block from Stark Street. Seven floors. Built in the fifties. It had a mix of legitimate, semi-legitimate, and not nearly legitimate tenants.

"Now what?" Lula asked. "Do we need to talk to Mr. Skoogie?"

"Yes. Skoogie laid out serious money for Waggle. He should be anxious to have him returned to the court."

I found on-street parking not far from Skoogie's office. I parallel-parked behind a Rollswagon that had seen better days, and Lula and I strolled into the lobby. Suite twelve was on the second floor at the end of the hall.

I opened the door to the suite and looked inside at a woman seated at a desk.

"Knock, knock," I said. "I'm looking for Leonard Skoogie."

"He isn't here," she said. "He's in L.A. for the rest of the week."

Photographs and posters covered almost every inch of wall space in the small room. There was a door off to one side which I assumed led to Skoogie's private office. The woman's desk was heaped with clutter, including an open box of Dunkin' Donuts.

"No," I said to Lula. "Don't even think about it."

"Hunh," Lula said.

"I'm actually looking for Victor Waggle," I said to the woman. "Perhaps you know him."

"Of course," she said. "Are you a fan? Would you like a signed photograph? We have them available for ten dollars."

"We already got a photograph," Lula said. "It got taken at the police station."

"Ours would be much nicer," the woman said. She pointed to the wall. "We have pictures of the band too."

Lula and I went to the wall and looked at the photographs.

"This sucker is in a band," Lula said. "I could recognize him by the snake tattoo. The other idiots in the band got spiders on their foreheads."

"Lead singer in Rockin' Armpits," the woman said. "Mr. Skoogie has high hopes for Victor."

"Yeah, us too," Lula said. "You know where we can find him?"

"They perform at the Snake Pit every Thursday and Friday."

"I guess that makes sense for someone that's got a snake tattooed on his neck," Lula said. "Where's it at?"

"Stark Street," the woman said. "It's easy to find. They always light the building with searchlights when the band is performing."

"I bet," Lula said.

"During the day, the building looks a little run-down," the woman said, "but I'm told it's very festive at night."

"It's only Tuesday," Lula said. "Suppose we want to find Victor before Thursday?"

"I'm afraid we're not allowed to release personal information on our clients," the woman said.

I gave her my business card. "Victor is in violation of his bond agreement," I said. "He missed his court appearance. We need to find him and get him rescheduled."

"Oh dear," she said. "It must have slipped his mind. Have you tried his cellphone?"

"He's not picking up."

"I'm afraid I don't know much about Victor. Often when our clients are in the early stages of their careers they tend not to have a permanent address."

"Why is that?" Lula asked.

"They haven't any money," the woman said. "I can give you a printout of our press release. It has the names of the four other band members. I imagine they would know where to find Victor."

"Mr. Skoogie is Victor's agent?" I asked.

"Agent and manager," she said.

I took the press release and thanked the woman. Lula and I left the office and returned to my car.

"I can't believe she didn't offer us a donut," Lula said. "That showed a less-than-gracious personality. I wouldn't trust someone who doesn't offer a guest a donut."

I didn't have a lot of thoughts about the donuts. My thoughts were about Skoogie and his interest in Victor Waggle. Hard to believe Skoogie's high hopes were sufficient to warrant putting up a five-figure bond for someone who went around stabbing people because he was having a bad day. Something was missing in the picture.

"I can't stop thinking about a donut now," Lula said. "It's stuck in my mind. I'm going to have to get a donut."

"It's almost ten. I'm heading for the deli. You can grab something to eat there."

"I'm impressed that you're taking your manager job seriously. What with all that's been happening, a lot of people wouldn't see this as having long-term career potential."

"I'm not interested in long-term career potential. I want to find Vinnie and Wayne Kulicki."

"So, you're making yourself the next target?"

"More or less."

"That could be a bad idea being that you're not exactly Ranger."

"No, but Ranger's going to help me. He's installing security cameras."

"I hate to be a party pooper, but I'm thinking security cameras aren't going to give you a lot of security. From my knowledge of this sort of thing, which mostly comes from *Star Trek,* it all happens pretty fast. You get vaporized and next thing you're having dinner with a Klingon."

"I'm going with the outside chance that it's not space aliens."

# CHAPTER SEVEN

I PULLED TO the curb in front of the deli and parked behind a Rangeman SUV. The deli door was unlocked, and Ranger's tech guy was inside, on a ladder. No surprise that he could let himself in. His name was Randy, and he was a master electrician, a pickpocket, a locksmith, a safecracker, and a sharpshooter. His work history prior to Ranger was south of the law.

"Good morning," Raymond said to Lula and me. "As you can see, we have a man in black working to bring us into the age of surveillance."

Lula went straight to the fridge. "Stephanie wants to have video for YouTube when she gets snatched up."

"She is a woman with vision," Raymond said.

"Where's that carrot cake from yesterday?" Lula asked. "I don't see it here."

"Bottom shelf," Stretch said. "If you eat it all you have to make a bakery run."

"I see two cakes down here," Lula said.

Stretch was setting up his prep area. "Yeah, like I said, if you eat it all you have to make a bakery run."

"Hunh," Lula said. "Smart-ass."

I walked through the kitchen to the back door and looked outside. There was no sign that anything out of the ordinary had taken place. The crime scene tape had been taken down. The lone shoe had been removed.

A man appeared at the edge of the parking area. It was Wulf. He crooked a finger at me and motioned me forward. I gave a single shake of my head, no. I mimicked his gesture, motioning him to come to me. He smiled. There was a flash of light, a burst of smoke, and he was gone.

I stepped back, closed the door, and sucked in some air. Hard not to get rattled by Wulf. I wasn't bothered by the theatrics. That was just Wulf having fun. I was bothered by the man. I knew him on a superficial level, as my drop-in friend Diesel's mysterious and complicated cousin. He was a man who tended to live in shadows and to come and go like thunder and lightning. And by "thunder and lightning" I'm not referring to his exit act, but by the disturbing magnetic, almost electric energy that surrounded him. He aroused my curiosity and simultaneously set off stranger-danger alarms. And I was a little freaked out that he was suddenly being seen in the two areas where people had vanished.

Everything seemed to be business as usual at the deli, so I called Connie and asked her to get me some information on the band members. Ten minutes later she texted back.

"I'm going to try to talk to the Armpit guys," I said to Lula. "I'll be back for the lunch rush. Do you want to stay here or come with me?"

"I'll come with you. Just in case you get beamed up off-site, I don't want to miss it."

Zigmund Klug was first on the list. He was nineteen and shared the same address as Victor Waggle. His parents lived in Arizona. He had no employment history. I moved him to last on the list.

Jaimie Rolls was living with his parents on Mayberry Street and was a pizza delivery specialist for Noohana's Pizza Emporium. I was familiar with Mayberry. It was tucked in behind the bonds office on Hamilton. It was a nice neighborhood of well-kept modest houses. I moved Jaimie to the top of the list.

"I heard about Noohana's," Lula said. "I saw it advertised on television the other day. They got emporiums all over the country, and if you order before noon and get them delivered after midnight, the pizza is only ninety-nine cents. I think that's because they must make them in China and ship them over here."

I found the Rolls house, and Lula and I went to the door. An older woman answered. Her hair was gray and cut short. Her skin was wrinkled and slack. She had a cigarette stuck to her lower lip and an overweight white cat under her arm.

"The cat tries to run out when you open the door," she said. "Either come in or go away. I can't hold this cat forever."

Lula and I stepped inside and closed the door. The woman put the cat down. It gave itself a quick couple licks, and walked away.

"We're looking for Jaimie Rolls," I said.

The woman squinted at us. "Are you hookers?"

"Not anymore," Lula said. "Only once in a while if I really need the money. Like sometimes when Macy's has a shoe sale."

I gave the woman my card. "We're trying to locate Victor Waggle," I said. "We thought Jaimie might be able to help us."

"Jaimie is in the cellar," the woman said. "It's his man cave. He goes down there to play with himself."

"Nice to see you're open-minded about it," Lula said.

"My daughter-in-law doesn't like it," the woman said, "but I don't see anything wrong with all those video games."

"Sure," Lula said. "I knew you were talking about video games."

The woman led us through the house to the cellar door. "Anyway, playing those games is better than when he tries to sneak the women in. Hookers and groupies and gropers. The worst is that mud wrestler Animal. He says he knows all these women because he's a rock star, but I think it comes from delivering pizza."

The cellar was unfinished, with beams and electrical wires overhead. The floor was concrete. Lighting was utilitarian.

The furnace and water heater took up one corner, and a lot of the rest of the space was given over to storage. In the midst of all this Jaimie had positioned a bedraggled couch, a large scarred wooden coffee table, and a television on a card table.

He was slouched on the couch in half-darkness, gamer remote in hand, concentrating on digitally killing people. He flicked a look at Lula and me and went back to his game.

"Ten bucks or a BJ for an autograph," he said.

"We're looking for Victor Waggle," I said. "Do you know where we can find him?"

"He'll be at the Snake Pit on Thursday."

"How about today?" Lula asked, moving in front of the television.

"Jeez, bitch," Jaimie said. "You got your fatness in front of my screen. I'm laying waste to the kingdom here. I'm like on a siege."

"Victor Waggle," I said. "Where is he?"

"He's nowhere. The dude is loose."

"He's 'loose.' What does that even mean?"

"It means he moves around. The bitches love him. They all want his seed."

Great. The moron with a snake tattooed on his neck is a seed spreader. Just what the world needs.

"How do you get in touch with Victor?" I asked.

"Sometimes he checks his text messages," Jaimie said. "Depends if he's having a good day or a bad day."

"Yeah," Lula said. "He stabs people on a bad day. And then he pisses on their dog."

"It was wrong of him to piss on the dog. We all called him on that," Jaimie said.

Lula and I returned to my car.

"I wouldn't want him delivering my pizza," Lula said. "He was rude and unattractive."

Martin Kammel was next up. He was a barista at Julio Coffee on State Street. His address was 415 Stark Street, apartment 3B. That was the fourth block of Stark and marginally safe.

"At least he *has* an address," Lula said. "And he's even got a good job, in spite of the spider on his forehead."

Julio Coffee was in a strip mall on the fringe of the state capitol complex. I parked in the strip mall lot, and Lula and I walked into the coffee shop. It looked a lot like a Starbucks except it was called Julio. Two men and three women were working behind the counter. None of them had a spider tattooed on their forehead. Lula ordered a Double Chocolate Chip Frappuccino, a Rice Krispies Treat, and a Morning Glory muffin. I ordered a Caramel Frappuccino.

"I was hoping Martin would be here today," I said to the woman who took my order.

"He's off today," she said. "He'll be here tomorrow."

"Are we going to his apartment now?" Lula asked me.

"No. There's not enough time for that. We'll go after the lunch rush."

■ ■ ■

Lula and I got back to the deli a little before noon, and people were already lining up outside. I opened the front door, and they followed me in. Raymond was at the fry station. Dalia was on the phone, taking down an order. Stretch was working at the prep table. Hal was standing behind Stretch. Hal was the elephant in the room. He's the size of a Volkswagen bus and not built to fit in a galley kitchen.

"Randy has all the cameras installed and working," Hal said to me. "And I'm supposed to stay here and make sure nothing bad happens to you."

"Very thoughtful but entirely unnecessary," I said. "I'll be okay. I even have a gun in my bag."

"I'm not supposed to let you out of my sight," Hal said. "Ranger won't be happy if I disobey orders. And it's not good when Ranger isn't happy."

"I can't work like this," Stretch said. "You gotta get Stegosaurus out of the prep area. And I need a sandwich maker."

"I'm up," Lula said. "Where's my hat? Where's my apron? Where's the hot sauce?"

I moved Hal into a corner, and I joined Lula.

"I'm getting the hang of this," Lula said. "I need turkey. Get me more turkey. And put mayo on this roll for me. And add some pickles."

"Wait," I said. "This is an order for ham and cheese."

"Say what?"

"You have to look at the ticket. You can't just give them *anything*."

"This here's Surprise Day. It's my new promotional idea. You order something and then you get a surprise. This guy's surprise is a turkey sandwich. Give me some of that green stuff."

"That's wasabi."

"No shit. I'm gonna wasabi the heck out of this sandwich."

"Where's my ham and cheese?" Stretch yelled. "Where's my pastrami on rye?"

"Keep your shirt on," Lula said. "I'm working under harsh circumstances. I can't find no more turkey."

"Fries are up," Raymond said. "Rings are up."

Stretch took the wasabi turkey from Lula, sliced it in half, and sucked in air.

"Damn," he said. "I cut off part of my finger."

I looked over and blood was all over his white chef's jacket, dripping off his finger onto the cutting board.

"Somebody get a Band-Aid," Lula said. "This boy needs a Band-Aid."

Stretch calmly picked something off the cutting board and stuck it to his bloody finger. He wrapped a paper towel around it all, took a Band-Aid from Raymond, secured the towel with the Band-Aid, and held his hand above his head.

"No big deal," he said. "I've done this before."

"Yes, this happens many times," Raymond said. "He must go to get his finger stitched back on now."

Hal was standing next to me. His eyes rolled back into his head, and he crashed to the floor.

"This big man just fell to the floor," Raymond said.

"He faints when he sees blood," I said. "He'll come around."

"I must return to my fry station," Raymond said. "I have many orders of onion rings that must be done to perfection."

"Take Stretch to the emergency room to get stitched up," I said to Lula. "Hal and I will take over here."

Everyone looked down at Hal. Lula toed him with her Louboutin knockoffs. Hal opened his eyes and blankly stared at the ceiling.

"What?" Hal said.

"You fainted," I told him. "Stay down until I get things cleaned up."

"Okay," Hal said. "Don't tell Ranger."

Dalia and I scrubbed everything with soap and bleach. I changed out the cutting board. I got Hal to his feet.

"Are you any good at making sandwiches?" I asked him.

"Yeah. I make good sandwiches. The trick is to put the mustard on the meat side and never use lettuce. Lettuce is for sissies."

I got him dressed up in a hat and apron and handed him a takeout order for six people.

"You do the takeouts, and I'll do the table orders," I told Hal.

He looked at the slip of paper. "No problem. I can do this, but there's no sliced turkey in the container labeled TURKEY."

"Don't worry about it. This is Surprise Day. Be creative."

# CHAPTER EIGHT

THE DELI WAS empty by two o'clock. I suspected most of the customers would never return. I did my best, but I was at the bottom of a learning curve. I had mustard in my hair, ketchup on my shirt, my workstation was a mess, and the floor was a health hazard.

"It is a very good thing that Stretch is not here to see this disgrace," Raymond said. "He would poop himself."

"Let's just clean up and move forward," I said.

I was praying that Stretch would be able to work the dinner shift. The dinner menu included hot sandwiches that involved gravy and melted cheese. This was way beyond my culinary skills.

"The dinner customers will be easier to please," Raymond said. "You can hide the ugliness of your sandwich making under a generous portion of gravy. They will not know what they are eating."

"I don't know how to make gravy," I said.

"You do not *make* gravy," Raymond said. "Gravy comes in five-gallon tubs. You might not have noticed them because the gravy tubs are very similar to the tubs of rice pudding and lard. In fact, once when Stretch was very stoned he gave a woman a dish of lard in place of the rice pudding. It was extremely funny."

I thought this must be fry-cook humor. And I hoped he never told that story to Lula because she took her rice pudding seriously.

The kitchen was almost clean when Lula and Stretch returned. Stretch had a bandage wrapped around his finger. Lula was carrying a grocery bag.

"We would have got back sooner, but we stopped for turkey and stuff," Lula said. "How'd lunch go?"

"Lunch was great," I said. "Easy peasy."

"Yes," Raymond said. "I was a frying maniac."

Dalia rolled her eyes and continued with her floor mopping.

"How bad is your finger?" I asked Stretch.

"It's okay," he said. "I just chopped the tip off. They were able to stitch it back on. I've done worse."

"Once he dropped the cleaver on his toe," Raymond said. "That was a bad time."

"Are you able to work?" I asked him.

"Cutie pie, if I had a dollar for every time I sliced off part of a finger I'd be a rich man."

"Okay then," I said. "I'm going to leave for a while. I'll be back to help with the dinner trade."

"I'll go with you," Lula said.

"Me too," Hal said.

I didn't mind this arrangement because if I got lucky and ran across Victor Waggle, Hal would be useful. He had blond hair styled in a buzz cut, a peaches-and-cream complexion, and enough muscle to stop a freight train. Plus, he could be the wheel man, and I would get to ride in a nice clean Rangeman SUV that gobbled up gas bought by Rangeman.

"Where are we going?" Hal asked.

"The fourth block of Stark Street," I said. "I want to talk to Martin Kammel."

"Hey, I know that dude," Hal said. "He's lead guitar with Rockin' Armpits."

I had a moment of blank brain. Hal knew Rockin' Armpits.

"I have one of their CDs. I got it signed," Hal said.

"One of the Armpits, Victor Waggle, is FTA," I said. "The only address he gave is a brick building that's full of bullet holes and gang graffiti. It's at the end of Stark."

"That sounds like the Snake Pit," Hal said. "I don't think anyone lives there. It's gutted inside. Only thing in it is a stage. I don't think there's even any plumbing."

"Is it safe to go there?"

"I wouldn't go there unless the band was performing. They

bring in lighting, and if you pay to park no one will steal your car. That's how they make their money . . . on the parking. And there's a big drug market. Once in a while someone gets shot, but aside from that it's pretty safe."

"And you go to this?"

"I used to date a girl who was all into Rockin' Armpits. We went to a couple Thursdays at the Pit. I haven't been there lately."

It never occurred to me that Hal might have a life beyond Rangeman. He was a nice guy, but he looked like he ate kale and raw meat, and his sole recreation was skinny-dipping in the ocean in January.

Hal cut across the center of the city, turned onto Stark Street, and parked on the fourth block. Kammel's building was a narrow four-floor walkup. The stairwell was dark and smelled like urine and burrito. There were two units on the third floor. I rang the bell for 3B.

"I don't hear no bell ringing," Lula said. "I think his bell is broken."

I knocked on the door. No answer. I knocked again. Nothing.

"Maybe you didn't knock loud enough," Lula said. "He could be hard of hearing being that he plays in a band. He might not be wearing his hearing aid."

"Let me try," Hal said.

Hal pounded on the door, and the door splintered around the lock and popped open.

"Oops," Hal said. "My bad."

A tall, skinny guy with a lot of curly black hair and a spider tattooed on his forehead looked out at us.

"Hey," he said, "you broke my door."

"Sorry," Hal said. "It was an accident."

"No big deal," Spider Head said. "I'm just crashing here. It isn't really *my* door."

"Martin Kammel?" I asked.

"Yeah."

I gave him my card. "I'm looking for Victor Waggle. He missed his court date and he needs to reschedule."

"This is about pissing on the dog, right? We all told him he shouldn't have done that."

"He also stabbed two people," I said.

"That was an accident. He was on a bad trip and got confused," Kammel said. "Like, that could happen to anybody, right?"

"It wouldn't happen to me," Lula said. "Where can we find Waggle?"

"No one knows where to find him," Kammel said. "He's GhostMan. He's in the wind."

"Let's break it down," I said. "Where does GhostMan sleep?"

"I don't know," Kammel said. "He travels light and he moves around."

"He's homeless," I said.

"Home is a state of mind," Kammel said. "Some people carry their home with them." He thumped his chest. "In their heart."

"Is that where your home is?" Lula asked him.

"Naw," he said. "I'm shacked up here with a crazy bitch."

We left Kammel and went back to the Rangeman SUV.

"That was an unsatisfying experience," Lula said. "We didn't find out anything, and he didn't even look like a rock star."

I checked my notes. "We have one last band member. Russel Frick. He's a lot older than the rest of the band. Works as a bagger at Food Stuff."

"I remember Frick," Hal said. "He's *real* old. Someone told me he plays with Armpit because he's the only guy they could find with his own drum set."

"Food Stuff is on Brunswick Avenue," I said. "Let's see if Frick is bagging today."

Hal took Pennington Avenue to Brunswick Avenue and headed north. Food Stuff was part of a strip mall just past the medical center. It was a warehouse-type supermarket that was locally loved for its double-coupon days. What it lacked in feel-good cozy it made up for in cheap. My kind of store.

We parked in the lot, and Lula grabbed a shopping cart on the way in.

"Why the cart?" I asked.

"I might see something I need. This here's a good store. They have a bakery that sells day-old stuff that's as good as new. And I hear they have excellent rotisserie chicken."

"We aren't shopping. We're working."

"Yeah, but this will only take a minute. You can go talk to the old guy, and I'll scope out the store."

I watched Lula swing her ass down an aisle, and I turned to Hal. Hal was a godsend. He knew the band. He recognized the members, and if I didn't find Waggle by Thursday, he would go to the Snake Pit with me.

"Do you see Frick?" I asked him.

"Yep. He's working with the next-to-last checker. He's the guy with the long gray hair. He's wearing the Spider-Man T-shirt."

I approached Frick and introduced myself. "I'm looking for Victor Waggle," I said.

"Aren't we all," Frick said. "He owes me money."

"I understand you and Waggle are bandmates."

"Rockin' Armpits," Frick said.

He stuffed milk and orange juice into a bag, added deli meats, cheese, and topped it off with a loaf of bread.

"You're a good bagger," Hal said to Frick. "You put all the heavy things in first, and you put the bread in last. I hate when baggers don't pay attention and the bread gets smushed."

"It's a skill," Frick said. "I have a good eye for fitting everything in."

"About Victor Waggle," I said. "Do you know where I can find him?"

Frick put the bag of groceries in a woman's cart and set a new empty bag on the shelf in front of him. "I don't think Victor has an address. He's like water. He flows into the empty space. He could be hanging out in a condemned building, or he could be living the good life, playing house with a groupie. I'm sure he'll be at the Snake Pit on Thursday. I've been with Armpit for a year, and Victor's never missed a gig."

"Is this your full-time job?" I asked Frick. "Can you make a living doing this?"

"I was an accountant for forty-three years," Frick said. "I retired two years ago, and now I do whatever I want."

"Playing the drums and bagging groceries?"

"Yeah, I get to meet people, and I make some spare change. Gives me something to talk about on my Facebook page."

"Do you ever hang out with Victor?"

"No. Victor isn't exactly intellectually stimulating. I think he hangs with Ziggy sometimes. Probably it's more like Ziggy follows Victor around when he can find him. Ziggy is needy. He's kind of lost."

Lula rushed up to the checkout with her cart. "I got us some good bargains. I got a birthday cake for a dollar. It says 'Happy Birthday, Larry, Ken, and Stanley,' but nobody came to pick up their cake, so it was on the sale table." She turned her attention to Frick. "This here's the band guy?"

"I'm on drums," Frick said.

"Aren't you kind of old?" Lula asked.

"Yeah," Frick said. "Aren't you kind of fat?"

"I'm not fat," Lula said, "I'm excessively proportioned. It goes with my extra-large personality. Do you know where we can find Victor?"

"No."

"Then I'm checking out and eating my cake. I need one of them plastic forks. Hell, forks for everyone."

We returned to the deli just before the rush-hour surge. Dalia was setting the tables, and Raymond and Stretch were working in the kitchen.

"I'm almost done with prep," Stretch said. "I need someone on the phone and someone on sandwiches."

"I'm all about the sandwiches," Lula said. "I'm the sandwich queen. Get out of my way 'cause here comes Lula."

"Hal can do the phone orders," I said.

"Hal doesn't fit in the kitchen," Stretch said. "Why can't you do the phone orders?"

"I'm the manager. I'm going to manage."

Mostly I was going to look around. I now had a monitor by the register, and I could pull up three views. Two views were of the parking area and dumpster, and one was of the deli interior. It was all being recorded and fed to the Rangeman control room, but I could see it live. I wanted to be able to watch the monitor, and I wanted to watch the customers. Managers disappeared quickly. There had to be someone on the inside. Either the snatcher or someone associated with him was a regular in the deli. And I wasn't ruling out Raymond and Stretch.

Two men came in and went to the takeout counter. They were wearing wrinkled suits and had their dress shirts unbuttoned at the neck. Commuters fresh off the train. They looked at Hal and hesitated for a moment. Hal was in black Rangeman fatigues with a Glock at his hip.

"Um, is everything okay here?" one of the men asked.

"Yeah," Hal said. "What's up? You want a sandwich?"

They ordered and took a step back. A woman rushed in and went to takeout. She looked at Hal, rolled her eyes, and did a small head shake. Like, what next? Hal took her order and turned to help Lula.

Dalia seated a couple and put their order in. I stepped around to the register to look at the monitor. Nothing going on by the dumpster. So far, I didn't recognize anyone as a repeat customer. A family came in. Mom and dad and two kids. They took a booth.

After an hour, everyone was pretty much looking the same. Men and women in rumpled suits, lining up for takeout. Families with restless kids looking for fast food. An occasional senior couple sometimes with another senior couple on a night out. No one looked like a killer or a space alien. Not a single Klingon in the room.

When someone complained about their sandwich, Dalia sent Hal to apologize, and that ended the sandwich dispute. Takes a special person to argue with a 250-pound guy packing a Glock.

It was almost eight o'clock when a man sauntered in and sat in a booth. I remembered him from yesterday. He'd come in at about the same time and ordered takeout. He was built like a bulldog and had short-cropped curly red hair.

“Who’s the big muscle man behind the counter?” the red-haired guy asked Dalia. “Is he the new manager?”

“No,” Dalia said. “Stephanie is the new manager.”

Red Hair looked over at me, and my heart skipped a beat. I forced a smile and gave him a little finger wave. He stared at me for a long moment before looking down at his menu.

So, here’s the thing. I’m not actually very brave. And I’m not skilled at solving crimes. Truth is, I have no business hanging myself out like this. And yet, here I am. Stephanie Plum, manager, sitting duck, idiot.

Dalia put her order in to the kitchen, and I pulled her aside.

“Who is the red-haired guy?” I asked.

“His name is Mike. I don’t know his last name. He pays with cash. Started coming in a couple months ago. He comes in late, and he always gets an extra side of slaw.”

Mike ate his meal, put some cash on the table, and left. I followed him to the door and watched him walk down the street. He turned at the corner and was gone from view. I ran after him, but by the time I got to the corner he’d disappeared. I waited for a few minutes to see if a car drove away from the curb. When no one did I assumed Mike lived in one of the row houses that lined both sides of the street.

I turned to go back to the deli and bumped into Wulf. He’d been standing inches behind me without my knowledge.

I yelped in surprise and jumped away.

“What the heck?” I said.

The sun was setting, and the whites of Wulf's eyes were very white in the semi-darkness. His voice was soft when he spoke.

"Return to the deli," he said. "Close up for the night, but don't go out the back door."

"Have you been following Mike?"

"No. I've been following you. We're both on a mission, and you have a knack for unwittingly stumbling across your prey."

"And we're both looking for the same man?"

"It's possible. It's necessary for me to leave for a short time. Until I return you are on your own, so be very careful."

Wulf stepped away and swept his arm out in a wide arc. There was a flash of light, some smoke, and he was gone.

"I *hate* when you do that!" I yelled after him. "It's freaky."

I stayed in place for several minutes, hoping to catch another glimpse of Mike or Wulf. Neither reappeared, so I walked back to the deli.

Raymond and Stretch were standing outside, smoking weed.

"It is good to see you," Raymond said to me. "You left very abruptly and didn't return, and we thought you might have fallen victim to the manager snatcher."

"Why are you out here? Why aren't you inside, working?"

"There are no more customers," Raymond said. "We are on a mental health break. We will clean everything perfectly when we are sufficiently relaxed."

I pushed through the door and found Dalia wiping down tables and Lula eating pie with Hal.

"This is a good job," Hal said. "We don't get pie at Rangeman. He doesn't want us to get fat."

Raymond and Stretch waltzed in, and we all got busy scrubbing down the kitchen. Almost an hour later, the kitchen was clean and Stretch had taken inventory and passed his list on to his vendors. Bags of garbage were lined up in the hall that led to the back door.

"Someone needs to take the garbage out to the dumpster," I said.

"I'd do it," Lula said, "but I don't want to be on video being the garbage girl. It would be unflattering."

"And I would do it, but I cannot lose my shoe," Raymond said. "I must wear two shoes at all times."

We all went to the back door. I opened the door, and we looked out. The parking area was lit by new floods installed by Rangeman.

Stretch picked up a garbage bag and flung it at the dumpster. It hit on the top corner and burst, spewing garbage onto the pavement. Two raccoons and a pack of rats as big as barn cats suddenly appeared and ransacked the mess. We all jumped back, and I closed and locked the back door.

"Okay then," I said. "Everyone takes a bag of garbage home with them."

"It might not make it all the way to my home," Raymond said.

"As long as it's not in the deli," I told him. "Try to get it at least a block away."

Lula and I set our bags of garbage in the trunk of my car, I locked the front door to the deli, and I drove Lula back to the bonds office to get her car. I made a brief stop at Giovichinni's dumpster to deposit the garbage, and I noticed Hal was following me.

I dropped Lula off and texted Morelli, telling him I still had both of my shoes, and I was on my way home. Maybe we could get together tomorrow. He texted me back a thumbs-up.

Hal was still behind me when I parked in the lot attached to my apartment building. He got out of his SUV and walked me to my door. He waited until I was in and the lights were on and I told him everything was okay.

"Thanks for keeping me safe today," I said.

"No problem," he said. "I got pie."

I waved him off and locked my door. I said hello to Rex and gave him a couple Froot Loops.

"The escort home was overkill," I said to Rex. "You have nothing to worry about. We're perfectly safe here." Especially since there was probably a Rangeman guy sitting in a patrol car in my lot, taking over for Hal. Ranger could sometimes be obsessive.

# CHAPTER NINE

LULA WAS AT the window when I got to the office. It was a little after nine A.M. and the single Boston Kreme donut was long gone.

"I see you're being followed," Lula said. "This is the second day in a row you've had a Rangeman escort."

I blew out a sigh. "Ranger is in full-on protective mode."

"It doesn't look like Hal in the car."

"Hal's shift doesn't start until the deli opens at ten."

"What the heck is this thing going on between you and Ranger?" Lula asked. "He gives you cars and security escorts and you get to stay in his personal Batcave when you want. I know he likes you but dang, you must be really good at something we don't know about."

I thought it was just the opposite. I'm not really good at

*anything.* I'm like an inept pet. Beloved but pretty much a disaster. And in spite of this, or maybe *because* of it, there's a lot of festering sexual attraction. Mostly the attraction goes unfulfilled, which I suspect contributes to the intensity of the festering.

"Do you notice anything different about me?" Lula asked.

Connie looked over at her. "Is your hair a different color?"

Lula changed her hair so often it was hard to remember from one day to the next.

"It's called Metallic Magenta," Lula said. "And I had Shanika brush it out to full volume."

I had to admit, the hair was spectacular. It looked like her head was a brilliant sunset that had exploded.

"I went to get it done first thing this morning so I'd be all set for going to the Snake Pit tonight," Lula said. "I'm all about Rockin' Armpits now that I'm a personal friend of the drummer, and the pizza guy, and what's-his-name from the coffee shop."

Crap! It was Thursday. Rockin' Armpits was at the Snake Pit tonight. I blew out another sigh. The day was going so good until I remembered this. I'd slept in. I'd had a luxurious shower. I'd had a second cup of coffee with a strawberry Pop-Tart. The sun was shining.

Now I was back to bounty hunter reality. Thursday had arrived. I told myself that I should be happy. I needed the money, and this was my best shot at getting Victor Waggle. Problem was, I knew it was also an opportunity for epic failure. I would have to attempt a takedown at the Snake Pit. There would be a lot of people in a small space. Some of those people would be scary. Many of them would be armed. Most of them would be high. I would want to create the least possible disturbance. That meant I would need to make my capture before or after the performance. And that meant I needed to be familiar with the stage area.

At least I had Hal. He was big, and he knew his way around the Snake Pit, and he actually had some skills. Like he probably knew how to shoot his gun and sucker punch a guy in the throat. Me, not so much.

"Looks like it's a good thing we've got the job at the deli," Lula said to me. "Otherwise we wouldn't have anything to do. You let Annie Gurky slip through your fingers, and you got Wayne Kulicki snatched. So now the only FTA we have left is Victor Waggle."

"Do we have any new cases?" I asked Connie.

"No," Connie said. "Maybe something will come in later today."

"I tell you it's a sad day in Trenton when there's so little crime that us bounty hunters are out of work," Lula said. "What's this town coming to? I think it's all because of those damn tax cuts. People don't have to steal and deal drugs no more."

"Drug dealers don't *pay* taxes," I said to Lula.

"Say what?"

"It's illegal to deal drugs, so drug dealers don't declare income."

"Hunh, I hadn't thought of it like that," Lula said.

"Let's go take a look at the Snake Pit before we open the deli."

I cut across town, turned right onto Stark, and cruised past the hookers, the gangbangers, and the stoop sitters. I reached the first block of war-zone buildings and looked for any indicators that one of them was the Snake Pit. I hit the second block and slowed when I approached Waggle's address.

"There's only one building standing here," Lula said. "This has to be where the band plays."

I didn't see any activity in the area. No cars. No people. No lighting equipment. No marauding packs of feral cats.

"I guess they set everything up last minute," Lula said.

I looked in my rearview mirror. The Rangeman SUV was still on my bumper. This gave me a warm, fuzzy feeling. I wasn't on my own in no-man's-land. I cut off Stark at the end of the block and headed for the deli.

Lula and I were the first to arrive. Hal pulled in just as I was opening the door. Stretch and Raymond wandered in minutes later. I flipped the lights on, Lula unlocked the back door for the provisions delivery, Raymond went to the fry station. The phone rang, and Hal took the first order of the day. We were settling into a work rhythm. This scared the bejeezus out of me. I didn't want to settle into a work routine here. This wasn't my dream job. Truth is, I didn't have a dream job in mind. I just knew *this* wasn't *it*. This job was even *less it* than my job as a bounty hunter. I thought after a couple weeks of working at this job it might be a relief to get abducted.

Lula had decided to wear her 'ho leathers as an accompaniment to her massive magenta hair. She was stuffed into over-the-knee black stiletto-heeled boots, a tight black leather skirt that barely covered her hoo-ha, and a black leather bustier that was struggling to contain her triple-D boobs. When she stood next to Hal in his Rangeman uniform they looked like they were working the lunch shift for S&M Deli.

A horn blared from the back lot, telling us the provisions truck had arrived. Raymond grabbed the clipboard hanging by Stretch's station and went to check off the supplies. There were several companies that made deliveries to the deli. The main provisioner, Central GP, came daily. Twice a week we received frozen foods. Twice a week the laundry was collected and returned by Kan Klean. And twice a week a Berger's Bits butcher shop truck delivered meat that wasn't frozen or pre-packaged. The only fish on the menu was tuna that came from a big restaurant-sized can.

Frankie drove the Central GP truck that brought us paper products, condiments, canned goods, baked goods, fresh produce, packaged lunch meats, dairy, and weed. My understanding was that the more exotic controlled substances were a special order. I personally don't do drugs. I have enough trouble making smart decisions when I'm clean and sober.

"We have received everything we asked for," Raymond said

when the truck pulled away. "I will put all these things in their proper place."

"It's Thursday," Stretch said. "Bonus day. Did Frankie leave us anything interesting?"

"Yes, I have some blue pills," Raymond said.

Stretch looked over at the bottle of pills. "What are they?"

"Frankie didn't know. Frankie found them in the pocket of a dead man. He was one of the line cooks for the East Street Banana Kitchen. Frankie carried a five-gallon container of rice pudding into the walk-in refrigerator and found the cook. He said even in his dead condition the man looked excessively happy, so he thinks the blue pills might be excellent."

"Have you tried them?"

"No," Raymond said. "I'm currently in an agitated state from many uppers. It would not be a good test of the happy pills if I tried them in my present condition."

We made it through lunch with fewer than normal complaints, and several diners took selfies with Lula and Hal.

"This is most interesting," Raymond said. "We have become a theme deli. I have some black leather chaps in my closet for special occasions that I might wear tomorrow. They would be appropriate for the fry station because they only expose my butt cheeks. I would not be in jeopardy of getting splatter burns on my sensitive frontal private areas."

I glanced over at Raymond. "If you wear chaps tomorrow, I'll turn you in to immigration."

"That would be cruel," Raymond said.

"Making me look at you in chaps would be cruel," I said.

"Not so," Raymond said. "I have firm butt cheeks with silky smooth skin. I am excellent to see in chaps."

"I'd be willing to take a look," Lula said. "Hell, I'll look at anything."

Stretch snapped on rubber gloves and lined up six roasted chicken breasts for slicing. "I'd sooner pour bleach in my eyes."

Hal looked like he was ready to get in line for the eye bleach.

Connie called. "You need to come to the office," Connie said. "Now."

"What's up?" I asked.

"Just get back here."

"I'm wanted at the bonds office," I said to Lula.

"I'll go with you," Lula said. "There's no one wanting sandwiches now."

"I'll drive," Hal said.

# CHAPTER TEN

SHADES WERE DOWN, the CLOSED sign was in the window, and the door was locked when we got to the office. I knocked on the door, and Connie opened it a crack and looked out.

"Thank goodness, you're here," she said. "I have a . . . situation."

We stepped inside and gave a collective gasp. Vinnie was standing in the middle of the room. He was buck naked, and he was swaying back and forth, back and forth.

"I can tell you right off I'd rather be looking at Raymond's butt cheeks," Lula said.

"I found him standing by the trash can in the parking lot," Connie said. "He was just standing there, swaying."

His eyes were completely dilated, his mouth was open, and he was drooling.

"What happened to you?" I asked him.

"I don't think he can talk," Connie said. "I think he might be drugged."

"This looks to me like the work of aliens," Lula said. "I bet they sucked out his brain."

"Did you call the police?" I asked Connie.

"No. I only called you. I wasn't sure what to do with him. I was hoping he would come around."

"We should call Lucille," I said.

"Yeah, and tell her to bring some clothes on account of her husband is in his altogether," Lula said.

We all stared down at Vinnie's foot. It was in his shoe.

"I guess I could amend that to his almost altogether," Lula said. "You gotta respect an alien that has the decency to return a man in his shoe."

"Vinnie!" I yelled. "Blink if you can hear me."

"Yuh," Vinnie said without blinking. "Yuh, yuh."

I called Morelli. "I need you to come to the bonds office," I said. "Now."

There was a beat of silence. "Can you be more specific?"

"I don't want to ruin the surprise."

"Are you naked?"

"No, but you're in the ballpark."

"I'll be there in a couple minutes."

"What's that mark on Vinnie's forehead?" Lula asked.

I leaned in and looked at the mark. "It's a number," I said. "It looks like it's been tattooed on. Vinnie is number thirty-seven."

"I saw that in a movie," Lula said. "The aliens tattooed numbers on people they abducted, so they could keep track of them after they sucked their brains out. The aliens were breeding the humans like cattle. Every morning they would collect the sperm from the brainless males and then they would use a turkey baster to impregnate the females. It was a product of the adult film industry, but it had some thoughtful content."

Hal was looking up at the ceiling and down at his shoes, trying not to stare at naked Vinnie.

"Maybe Vinnie wants a donut," Lula said to Connie. "You have any left?"

Connie took the donut box out of the trash. "There's one left," she said. "It's a little stale but it looks okay."

Lula offered it to Vinnie. "Would Vinnie like a donut?"

"Yuh," Vinnie said. He snatched the donut from Lula and shoved it into his mouth. There was a lot of chewing and drooling, and through it all he kept swaying. A chunk of donut fell out of his mouth, onto the floor. He didn't seem to notice.

"Good Vinnie," Lula said. "Good boy." She turned to me. "Someone should take him outside to tinkle."

"He's not a dog!" I said.

"They did that in the film," Lula said. "The brainless males were like dogs. They went outside to tinkle and poop. They did the sperm collection inside. It was pretty interesting. They had a lot of different ways to go about getting the sperm. Do you want to know what they did?"

"No," Connie said. "Not without a glass of wine."

Hal made a sound like he was swallowing his tongue.

"Maybe some other time," I told Lula.

Morelli knocked once and came inside. He looked at me, and then he looked at Vinnie.

"Holy crap," Morelli said.

"Connie found him in the parking lot," I said. "He's got the other shoe on."

"Yeah, I noticed that right away," Morelli said. "That and the fact that he's naked and has a number tattooed on his forehead."

"I got a theory about that," Lula said.

"What's the theory about the dilated eyes and the drooling?" Morelli asked.

"He seems to be a little drugged," I said. "Maybe we should have him checked out."

"Can he talk?"

"Yuh," Vinnie said.

Morelli squelched a grimace. "Can he say anything besides 'Yuh'?"

"Not yet," I said. "We were hoping he would come around."

Morelli put a call in for an EMT transport.

A half hour later Vinnie was being wheeled into the ER, and Lucille was on her way to the hospital.

Morelli took me aside. "What's with the Rangeman guy?"

"I asked Ranger to install security cameras at the deli, and he decided I needed personal security as well. So, I have Hal."

"Lucky you. Is Hal watching the game with us tonight?"

"No game. I have a takedown tonight after I close at the deli. Hal's going to help."

"Do I want to know about this?"

"No."

Morelli kissed me on the forehead. "I have to get back to my desk to finish today's paperwork. Be careful tonight."

Connie stayed with Vinnie. Lula, Hal, and I went back to the deli. Raymond was alone in the kitchen when we walked in.

"Where's Stretch?" I asked.

"I have him locked in the pantry. He took some of the bonus pills, and he got very silly."

"*How* silly?" I asked.

"He is a little hallucinogenic. There was a moment when he was talking to his chef's knife, and I became concerned, so I bribed him into the pantry with a jar of mayonnaise, and then I locked the door."

"Is he in there with the knife?"

"No. I confiscated the knife. He and the knife appeared to be having a disagreement."

I went to the pantry and knocked on the door. No answer. I knocked again.

"Maybe he has fallen asleep," Raymond said.

I unlocked the door and peeked inside. Stretch was sitting on the floor, eating out of the mayonnaise jar with his finger. He looked up at me and giggled. I closed and locked the door.

"He's okay," I said.

Dalia rushed in. "Sorry I'm late," she said. "I had car trouble."

Several customers had come in behind her.

"We need someone to be the new Stretch," Raymond said. "I must tend to my fry station."

I blew out a sigh. "I'll do it. Give me a menu so I have a cheat sheet."

Dalia slapped an order onto the counter. "I've got a sixteen, and a thirty-two with extra cheese, and a number nine, hold the onions."

"A nine is a burger," Lula said. "Here's your roll. Put it on the grill with the burger. I got the sixteen."

Thirty-two was a chili dog. I could do that. I threw a hot dog on the grill with the burger.

Dalia put another order on the counter. "I need two number twelves and a side of fries," she said.

"I need fries," I yelled at Raymond. "And two twelves."

"I do not do twelves," Raymond said. "Twelve is a microwave."

Lula handed me a plate. "Here's my sixteen. You need to finish it off."

I stared down at it. "What is it?"

"It's a number sixteen," Lula said.

"Yes, but what is it?"

"It's egg salad on a croissant. I ran out of egg salad, so I mixed in some tuna salad. I figure it's all done with mayo, right?"

"It's not on a croissant."

"I thought it would go better on a hamburger bun."

I put lettuce, tomato, and some pickles on the plate and set it on the counter for pickup. I put the burger in the bun and plated it up with pickles and fries.

"Where's my thirty-two?" Dalia said.

"Coming!" I yelled.

I had the hot dog but no bun. The hot dog buns were still in the pantry. I ran to the pantry, opened the door, grabbed the package of buns, and ran back to my station.

"Order up," I yelled, throwing some chopped onions and chili on the hot dog.

"Fries for the twelve," Raymond said.

I had no idea what constituted a twelve. "I need something that looks like a twelve," I said to Lula. "I need two of them."

"There's no cheese on my extra cheese dog," Dalia said. "And I need a party Italian to go."

I turned and bumped into Stretch. He'd escaped from the pantry.

"Mary had a little lamb," he said. "Its fleece was white as snow." He looked up and stuck out his tongue like he was catching snowflakes.

Hal was watching from the end of the counter. "Do you want me to put him back in the pantry?"

"Can you make two twelves?" I asked Stretch.

"Yes," Stretch said. "I'm Princess Twilight Sparkle, and I can do anything because I ate the magic whiteness."

"First off, he isn't nearly Princess Twilight Sparkle," Lula said. "That happens to be my favorite Little Pony.

And what the heck is the magic whiteness? Is that some racial thing?"

"He ate a jar of mayo," I said. "The big one."

"That'll go through you like goose grease," Lula said. "We all might want to stand back in case . . . you know."

"I *am* Princess Twilight Sparkle," Stretch said. "I know because I can see inside my head, and it's rainbow colors." He pulled two cutlets out of the under-the-counter fridge. He put his nose to the cutlets and sniffed. "They smell like pink and green happiness," he said. "Pink and green is the best kind of happiness."

"So true," I said. "About the number twelve?"

Stretch put the cutlets into the microwave and gave them a minute while he sang a *la la la la* song. He added marinara sauce and cheese and gave it all thirty seconds. "Do you like my ponytail?" he asked me. "It's more rainbow color, and it's sprinkled with pixie dust so I can fly."

I looked over at Hal, and I mouthed, *Is he kidding*?

Hal grinned and shrugged.

"Would you like to see me fly?" Stretch asked.

"Maybe later," I told him. "Can you make a party Italian to go?"

"Yes, and I can catch the snowflakes on my tongue while I make it."

"Princess Twilight Sparkle can stay," I said to Hal. "Just don't let him near any knives."

▪ ▪ ▪

We hung the CLOSED sign on the door at nine o'clock. Mike was a no-show. Princess Twilight Sparkle was on the floor behind the register, sleeping off his blue pill hangover. Connie had reported that Vinnie was admitted to the hospital for observation. Seven garbage bags were lined up in the hall leading to the back door.

"What about all this garbage?" Hal asked.

"We'll take it out in the morning when the Central GP truck shows up," I said. "That seems to be a safe time."

"Not for me," Lula said. "I'm not going out that back door no matter what time of day it is. I don't want to end up being one of the brainless breeder women."

"Are you talking about the film where the aliens abducted people to raise them like cattle?" Raymond asked. "That was an excellent film. Thought provoking. And I was surprised at some of the methods they used to extract sperm. Some were shockingly innovative. Although many were labor intensive."

"My feelings exactly," Lula said.

I looked around. The place was a mess. Food on the floor. Mustard and ketchup smeared on workstations. Cheese melted onto the grill. Grease everywhere. It had been a nerve-racking, exhausting dinner shift. And now we were faced with the cleanup.

"Sometimes when we are coming down from the many

drugs we must take to make it through the night in this hellhole kitchen, we leave the cleanup to morning," Raymond said.

"Everyone in favor raise their hand," Lula said, raising her hand.

"That's okay with me," I said, "but we should at least shovel the food off the floor."

"It will be an easier job in the morning if you allow the roaches and rodents to eat their share," Raymond said. "I have had some experience in this area."

"Sounds like a plan to me," Lula said.

We roused Stretch and shuffled him out the door. Once we had him outside, we loaded him into the Rangeman SUV along with Lula and me. He lived within walking distance of the deli, but we didn't trust him to walk home. He no longer thought he was Princess Twilight Sparkle, but he looked like he was on the low side of smart. Hal parked, walked Stretch to his door, and turned him over to his roommate, Bucky.

"How'd that go?" Lula asked Hal.

"Bucky will keep an eye on him," Hal said. "It's kind of a shame the pill wore off. He was so happy being Twilight Sparkle."

"When will Armpit be playing?" I asked Hal.

"They're not the first band. They usually start around ten or eleven. They play for a couple hours and then another band takes over. Usually the Beggar Boys or the Howling Dogs."

"You know the Snake Pit," I said. "What's the best way to do this?"

"Everyone comes and goes from the left side of the stage," Hal said. "They keep a corridor sort of clear for the band people. And there's a door to the outside. I don't know what's out there. Probably a bunch of people hanging around. Maybe a parking area. I guess I'd wait until the band was done, and then I'd either take Victor down when he goes out the door, or I'd follow him when he leaves and wait for the right time."

"Will we be able to get to the stage door?"

"I don't know," Hal said. "I've never tried. Melton Street runs parallel to Stark. I'll drive down Melton and try to get a look at the back of the Pit."

We saw the lights when we were blocks away. Bright ambient light from floods in an area that was otherwise dark. Buildings were gutted and unoccupied for several blocks at this end of Stark. Streetlights had been shot out and never replaced. Car traffic was usually minimal here. Tonight, though, there was activity.

"Damn," Lula said. "This is lit up like Vegas. How come I didn't know about this? They got a party going here."

"It's an open-air drug fair," Hal said. "They sell stuff here that makes the blue pill Stretch took look like kids' candy."

Melton Street wasn't high-rent, but it wasn't Stark either. People lived on the end blocks of Melton. There were seniors sticking it out because they had no other place to go, homeless souls hunkered down in buildings that had been condemned, and runaway drugged-out kids sheltered in hallways and abandoned apartments.

Hal cruised down Melton and stopped when he thought he was behind the Pit.

"This isn't helping," Lula said. "I can't see past these broken-down buildings."

Tenement-style row houses were smashed together, blocking our view. We could see strobe lights flashing across the sky, emanating from Stark, but we couldn't see between the grimy, graffiti-covered structures.

There was on-street parking here, but no one dared leave a car unattended. This wasn't a problem for the residents because if you were unfortunate enough to need to live here, you for sure couldn't afford a car.

Hal turned at the corner and drove toward Stark. He stopped at a checkpoint, handed over a fifty-dollar parking fee, and was allowed to proceed and park wherever he could find a spot in the two-block area that had been cordoned off. He pulled into a slot, cut the engine, and got a windbreaker from the back seat. Cars were streaming in behind us. The people getting out of the cars were young. High schoolers. Millennials. The cars, for the most part, were new and compact. Clothes were a mix of early Britney Spears and Seattle grunge.

Hal shrugged into the windbreaker, hiding his Rangeman patch and holstered gun. Lula fluffed up her magenta hair and tugged her spandex skirt down over her ass. I followed behind, feeling like Frump Girl in my jeans and T-shirt and plain brown ponytail.

The parking area and the front of the warehouse were lit. Not quite as bright as daylight, but bright enough to buy and sell drugs, sex, and Snake Pit T-shirts.

Two garage bay doors had been rolled up, allowing people to enter and exit what had now become the Snake Pit. A band called the Romanian Slippery Unicorn was already onstage, blasting out music that was so bass-heavy I was getting heart arrhythmia. The lighting was lower inside. A cannabis and menthol vapor haze hung over the crowd.

Hal took point to get to the front, plowing through what appeared to be an army of stoner zombies. Lula followed Hal, waving her arms in the air, bobbing her head, and swinging her ass like she was on *Soul Train.* I stayed in Lula's wake.

We got close enough to see when Rockin' Armpits and Victor Waggle were about to take the stage. Hal changed direction and moved us left so we'd be in a good position when they finished playing and headed for the exit.

Hal watched the band and the crowd in full-on Rangeman protective mode. Lula took selfies, posted them for her Facebook friends, and looked like she knew what the band was playing. I focused on Victor Waggle and did shallow breathing, hoping to minimize the contact high.

At eleven-thirty I saw Victor look to the side of the stage and nod to someone. Hal saw it too and began to move us toward the side exit. Ten minutes later, the band played their last song, waved at the audience, and bounded off the stage. We made an effort to follow them but were stopped at the door.

Lula adjusted the girls and leaned forward. "Hold on here," she said to the doorman. "We're special friends of all them Armpits. We have a personal relationship. You can ask anybody, except for the little guy with the green hair. We don't know him personal. Furthermore, I've had a request from certain members of the band to pay a visit and work my magic. They gonna be unhappy if you don't let Lula through to work magic."

"Okay, you can go in," the doorman said. "But only you."

"No way," Lula said. "I don't go nowhere without my security detail. When you got talents like I got you need people around who know CPR and shit."

Most of Lula's boobs had jiggled out by now with only her massive nipples caught inside the bustier. The doorman was having a hard time looking past the trapped nipple to the security detail.

"Whatever," he said. "Maybe you want to save some of that magic for me."

"When I'm done with you, your dick will never be the same," Lula said. "I'll ruin you."

We all hurried through the door and looked around for Victor Waggle. Lighting was minimal, supplied mostly by Maglites and cellphone flashlights. There were thirty to forty people milling around in the small outdoor space. Some looked like the band about to go onstage next. Some looked like groupies and roadies. Some looked like event security. I spotted Russel Frick off to one side, packing his drum set into a cart.

"Hey," I said, "remember me?"

"Bounty hunter."

"Yeah. Is Victor here somewhere?"

"He went up front to find a meal ticket."

"How do I get up front from here?"

Frick pointed to the narrow alley between the buildings. "Follow the yellow brick road."

I grabbed Hal and Lula, and we ran down the alley to Stark. People were standing around talking, smoking, checking out street vendors. Victor Waggle was with several women in front of a food truck that was selling hot dogs. It looked like he was autographing photos.

We did a flanking maneuver and sneaked up behind him. I had my cuffs ready and was about to clap one on his wrist when one of the women yelled, *"PIG!"*

Victor whirled around, saw the cuff, and jumped away. One of the women kicked me in the knee, and two others pulled out guns.

"That's rude," Lula said to the woman who kicked me. "What's the matter with you? You don't kick sisters for no cause."

"I got lots of cause," the woman said. "I'm loaded with cause." And she kicked Lula.

Lula swung her purse and hit the woman square in the face, knocking her off her feet.

Someone squeezed off a couple shots that took out a piece of

Lula's magenta hair before they embedded themselves in the hot dog truck. Everyone either hit the ground or ran for cover.

"I've been shot!" Lula screamed. "Lordy, someone help me. I've been shot."

"She just got you in the hair," I said.

Hal had the shooter by the back of her shirt. He was holding her at arm's length with her feet not touching the ground. He had her gun in his other hand.

"What do you want me to do with her?" he asked.

"Put her down. We lost Waggle. He ran when she started shooting."

Hal looked around. "It's going to be hard to find him now."

"We can try again tomorrow," I said.

"Not me," Lula said. "I'm not coming back here. These people have no respect. I got shoved and kicked and shot at. And I got my hair ruined." She felt around where her hair had been shot off. "It's not like hair grows on trees," she said.

# CHAPTER ELEVEN

IT WAS FRIDAY morning. The sun was shining. My Rangeman escort was on my bumper. I was on my way to the bonds office.

I was going more out of habit than necessity. Realistically speaking, I only had one open file, and chances of making that capture this morning were close to zero—unless Victor Waggle staggered into the road in a drug-induced stupor and I accidentally ran over him.

Lula was eating the Boston Kreme donut when I walked in.

"I never expected to get the good donut today," Lula said to me. "It took me forever to figure out what to do with my hair. I couldn't get a salon appointment until tomorrow. Why are *you* late?"

"I didn't want to start my day."

"I hear you," Lula said. "I'm getting the feeling our life is going south. We're not having a lot of luck being bounty hunters, and the deli is turning into the kitchen from hell. I'm not even sure about my career as a sandwich maker anymore. I feel like I'm underappreciated by some of the customers."

"Maybe because they never get what they order."

"Yeah, but I'm giving them a unique culinary experience. It's called haute cuisine. I read about it in a magazine while I was waiting to get my nails done. I'm all about haute cuisine and haute couture. I bet I could haute couture the hell out of anyone in Trenton."

No doubt. At the moment, she was wearing a blond Farrah Fawcett wig, a fire-engine-red sequined tank top, a short spandex purple skirt that had metallic silver threads running through it, and five-inch silver platform heels.

"What's the word on Vinnie?" I asked Connie.

"He's supposed to go home today."

"Is he talking? Did he say what happened to him?"

"He's talking, but I don't think he can remember anything about his abduction. At least that's what he told Lucille. Morelli might know more."

I called Morelli and asked him about Vinnie.

"He seems to be healthy," Morelli said. "No signs of torture or abuse. Turns out the number on his forehead wasn't tattooed. It was put on with a marker pen. The last thing he remembers is getting out of his car in the parking area behind the agency. Toxicology reports haven't come back yet, but I'm sure they're going to find some sort of amnesiac drug in his system. He had needle tracks on his arm."

"And his shoe?"

"Clean, but, again, all the lab work isn't back."

"I wish you would solve this, because the deli job is getting old."

"I hate to pass this on to you, but we've got zip. We're counting on you to figure it out."

"Oh boy."

"I have to get back to my blood and guts job," Morelli said. "I'll see you tonight. We're still on for dinner at your parents' house, right?"

"Crap, I completely forgot. I have to work at the deli."

"I thought this was a birthday party for your sister."

"Double crap!"

I disconnected and looked at Lula. "I need to get a birthday present for Valerie."

"You forgot your sister's birthday, didn't you?" Lula said. "That's terrible. Shame on you."

"I have other stuff on my mind." Like staying alive.

"What are you going to get her?" Lula asked.

"I don't know. I hate the whole present thing. I never know what to get anyone."

"I give people gift cards," Lula said. "You could buy them in the supermarket. They're easy. There's gift cards for everything from Starbucks to Target and in between. I like them on account of the message they send. I figure it puts people on notice. A gift card says *I feel obligated to get you something, but I don't care enough to put any effort into finding just the right gift.* Gives people some idea of their place in your life, you see what I'm saying?"

"You gave me a gift card for Christmas," I said to Lula.

"Yeah," Lula said, "but I put some thought into which one to get you. I gave you a card for that big liquor store on Liberty Street."

"I'm heading for the deli," I said. "The kitchen needs cleaning."

"We need one of them cleaning services," Lula said. "You can't expect a sandwich artist like me to be scrubbing floors. I need to focus my energy in the direction of ham and cheese."

I wanted to focus my energy in the direction of turning the deli into a pile of smoldering cinders, but that wasn't going to help me find Wayne Kulicki.

"A cleaning service is a great idea," I said. "You're in charge of finding one. In the meantime, someone needs to scrape the grease off the grill and scoop up the dead roaches before we start serving lunch."

It was nine-thirty when we got to the deli. Stretch was already there, sitting on the sidewalk with his back to the front door. He stood when he saw me.

"Did I put sauerkraut on a number twenty-two?" he asked.

"Yes," I said. "And ketchup. You put ketchup on everything, including lemon meringue pie."

"I thought it needed a splash of color."

"You were in My Little Pony Land."

"It was my happy place," Stretch said.

"It wasn't *my* happy place," Lula said. "You were out there, whackadoodle. I take my sandwiches seriously, and I don't want some doper coming around adding extra condiments."

Raymond ambled down the street and nodded in greeting. "I'm hoping that when we open the door, the deli will be magically cleaned," he said. "I have it on very good authority that sometimes the tooth fairy has a light day and does these things."

"I'm hoping that's your sense of humor and not coming from something extra you put in your wake-up weed," Lula said.

Raymond did more head bobbing. "I have a very excellent sense of humor."

Hal drove up, my night-shift Rangeman guy drove off, and Hal parked in his spot behind my Nova. I plugged my key into the deli's front door, reached in and switched the light on, and we all waited outside for a moment while the roaches scurried out of sight.

The laundry pickup and delivery came at ten-thirty. The butcher truck came ten minutes later, and Central GP honked their horn in the back lot a little after eleven.

"Sorry I'm late," Frankie said. "Fridays are always nuts. Everyone ordering for the weekend. Except the deli. You get commuter trade here. Weekends not so much."

"I'm sure we're one of your smaller accounts," I said. "I'm surprised that you stop in every day. The other suppliers come twice a week."

"You're in between Munchers Italian and the Corner Grille. They get fresh bread daily, so it's no biggie for me to stop here."

Plus, he distributes drugs, I thought. Stretch and Raymond were good customers.

"I hear you've got a new menu," Frankie said. "How's it doing?"

"It's not exactly a new menu," I said. "It's mostly like the sandwich maker is overly creative."

"Who's making these sandwiches? Is it the big guy?"

"Hal? No, Hal is working the phone and keeping an eye on things."

"You mean, like, he's the manager now?"

"He's more like security."

"Yeah, you got a problem. It's gotta be scary to work here and wonder who's gonna be the next one to disappear and lose a shoe. I'm surprised this place is still in business."

"You know about that?"

"*Everyone* knows about that," Frankie said.

I signed the receipt for the day's delivery of rolls, paper towels, avocados, mayo, and a quart-size plastic bag labeled OREGANO.

"Who gets the oregano?" I asked Frankie.

"Raymond. It's for the French fries."

■ ■ ■

A news crew from one of the local television stations walked through the front door at one o'clock and began filming. They panned around the dining area and made their way back to the kitchen.

Raymond grabbed his bag of oregano and ducked down. "I must go to the little boys' room," he said. "Do not let my fry station go out of control."

Stretch and Dalia went about business as usual.

Lula ripped her apron off and adjusted the girls. "I bet they heard about my sandwiches," Lula said. "This could be the start of a big television career for me. I even got a name for my show. I'm gonna call it *Lula's Buns* on account of my best sandwiches are made on those smushy hamburger buns we get from the truck."

I wasn't nearly so excited about the television crew. My mind was racing down black roads of panic. I didn't want to announce to the world that I was the manager of the deli. I didn't want publicity that might bring in more customers when we could barely service our regulars. Plus, we had giant roaches, mutant rats, half the stuff in the fridge expired months ago, and there was green fuzzy stuff growing in the pantry. Raymond was probably flushing his oregano down the toilet, but God knows what everyone had in their lockers.

The television crew consisted of a cameraman, a reporter in

a wrinkled suit, and a guy who said he was the producer. The producer was wearing Jesus sandals and looked like he slept in a cardboard box under the bridge.

The reporter went directly to Lula. "How does it feel to be an Internet sensation?" he asked her.

Lula leaned forward. "Say what?"

"Yesterday you had twenty thousand likes on your YouTube video."

"I didn't post no video," Lula said.

"I saw it," Dalia said. "It was posted by a customer. It was titled 'S&M Sandwich Bitch,' and it was you in your black leathers, making sandwiches and cussing out Stretch."

"He was ruining my sandwiches," Lula said. "He was putting ketchup on everything. I take my sandwiches seriously."

"Who are you today?" the reporter asked Lula. "Are you Doris Day?"

"I could see you don't know much about Doris Day," Lula said. "If I was Doris Day I'd have on a pillbox hat and I'd be wearing a fluffy pink sweater. And anyways I'm always Lula. I don't do that *other people* shit." Lula looked at the camera guy. "Can I say 'shit' on television?"

"No," he said. "We'll have to bleep that out."

"That's too bad," Lula said. "I emoted it with real conviction. It could have been a good sound bite."

The reporter looked at the sandwich Lula was making. "What is this?" he asked.

"It's a chicken parm," Lula said.

"It doesn't look like a chicken parm."

"That's because without any extra charge I'm giving this person a chicken parm supreme à la Lula. I added bacon and brown gravy on account of everything is better with bacon and gravy."

The cameraman zoomed in on the supreme à la Lula.

"Order up," Stretch yelled. "Where's my chicken parm? Where are my fries?"

"There aren't any fries," I said. "Raymond is in the little boys' room. It might have something to do with the oregano."

"I need a number twenty-three and a number four," Dalia said.

The cameraman swung around to get a shot of Dalia and clipped Stretch's arm with his camera. The chef's knife got knocked out of Stretch's hand, fell to the floor, and impaled the producer's foot.

Time stood still for a full minute while everyone stared in shocked horror.

"Holy bleep," Lula said.

Stretch pulled the knife out of the guy's foot and blood spurted everywhere. The cameraman went in for a close-up, and Hal fainted. *Crash!*

"I need that chicken parm," Dalia said, "and table three wants apple pie."

"Chicken parm's up," Stretch said. "It's the plate that looks like diarrhea on bacon."

I wrapped a towel around the producer's foot, and Lula bound it up with plastic wrap.

"What's happening?" one of the customers asked. "What's going on?"

"We got a issue here," Lula told him. "Any of you people a podiatrist?"

No one was a podiatrist, so we scooped the producer up and helped him hobble out to the news van.

"Sorry about this," I said to the reporter. "I hope it won't reflect badly on the deli."

"Lady, with the reputation this deli is getting, a stabbing can only enhance it," the reporter said.

Hal was sitting in a booth when we got back inside, but he wasn't looking great. Lula gave him a number three with extra gravy and a glass of orange juice. Dalia took a mop to the blood on the kitchen floor. Stretch washed his chef's knife and poured bleach over it. We comped the checks for all the customers, and got Raymond out of the bathroom.

"Now we're all back to normal," Lula said. "I might take the time to get my nails done before the dinner rush, since I'm changing out my hair tomorrow. I'm liking this blond wig. And I might want to stay blond for a while so people can recognize me after I've been on television. I'm thinking I'll go blond and maybe I want some champagne nail varnish."

"I have to get Valerie a birthday present," I said. "And then I need to show up for a party at my parents' house. I'll get back to close, but I won't be here for dinner."

"No problem," Lula said. "We got it covered."

"What about Mr. Muscle?" Stretch asked. "Is he going to the party or can he work phones for us?"

"Do you mind working phones?" I asked Hal.

"If it's okay with Ranger, it's okay with me," Hal said.

"Where are you going shopping?" Lula asked. "Do you have ideas for Valerie?"

"I have no ideas. I thought I'd go to the mall and look around."

"That's the worst," Lula said. "That's like shopping death. You'd better take me with you. I'm good at shopping."

"I thought you were getting your nails done."

"I'll get them done tomorrow. I can see you need my help here."

Hal parked in the lot at Quaker Bridge Mall, and we all trooped into Macy's.

"What's Valerie's size?" Lula asked.

"I don't know. She's put some weight on since the last baby, and she doesn't discuss size."

"What about a scarf? A scarf fits all sizes."

"I don't think she's a scarf person."

"How could someone not be a scarf person? Everybody is a scarf person."

"I've never seen you wear a scarf."

"Yeah, but that's me. I don't like to wear something that takes attention away from my girls."

We wandered past the scarfs, handbags, and lingerie. Nothing jumped out at me as being perfect for Valerie and in my price range.

"Perfume?" Lula asked. "Candle?"

"Albert has allergies to certain scents."

We moved out of Macy's into the mall. Lula led the way, I followed Lula, and Hal followed me.

"Here's one of my favorite jewelry stores," Lula said. "They got the best fake diamonds. You can't tell the difference. And they got stuff that looks like it's old. It's the 'Family Heirloom' collection."

"Valerie doesn't wear jewelry anymore," I said. "The baby grabs it."

"They got an Arthur Murray Dance Studio here," Lula said. "You could give her dance lessons. Or how about a hat? You could get her name embroidered on it. They do it while you wait."

We all stopped and had giant pretzels and ice cream and went to the second level. We passed by Mr. Alexander's, Classy Nails, and a wig shop.

"There's a novelty store here that has all kinds of good stuff," Lula said. "They have about forty different kinds of vibrators. You could get Valerie one of those. What girl doesn't want a vibrator?"

Somehow, I couldn't see Valerie at the table, unwrapping a vibrator while my mother cut the birthday cake.

"There's a bookstore here somewhere," Lula said. "I've never been in it, but I saw it advertised. Maybe she would like a book."

"She has four kids," I said. "She hasn't got time to read."

"That's a shame," Lula said. "Everyone should read."

"Do you read?"

"No. But I think about it sometimes. Problem is, I go to a bookstore and there's so many books I get confused. So, I get coffee. I know what I'm doing when I order a coffee."

Hal looked like his feet hurt, and he would be thankful for a lobotomy.

"We've been walking around for hours," Lula said. "I'm out of ideas, and Hal and me need to get back to the deli."

"Suppose it was your sister," I said to Lula. "What would you get her?"

"That's easy," Lula said. "I'd get her one of them BeDazzler kits. They got them in that novelty store with the vibrators."

Done and done. We stopped at the card store on the way out of the mall, and I got a big gift bag, some pink tissue paper, and a card. I stuffed the BeDazzler into the bag, signed the card, and I was ready to party.

I called Ranger and told him I'd be with Morelli for Valerie's birthday dinner, so I was sending Hal back to the deli with Lula.

"I'm going to have to give Hal a combat bonus," Ranger said. And he disconnected.

# CHAPTER TWELVE

HAL WALKED ME to my parents' front door, and in the absence of Morelli, turned me over to Grandma Mazur. Morelli arrived twenty minutes later.

"Am I late?" he asked.

"No," I said. "I was early. Is there any new information on the shoe snatcher?"

"We have a medical report on Vinnie that suggests he was shot in the back with a dart gun. That's probably how he was taken down."

"Would a drug work that fast?"

"It could, depending on the drug used and the amount administered."

"Anything else?"

"No. He doesn't remember anything. We've canvassed both

neighborhoods multiple times and haven't found any witnesses. No one's heard screaming or shots fired. If the bad guys are driving the victims away, they must be using a commonly seen car that's completely unmemorable."

"Vinnie is the odd man," I said. "He's the only one who was taken from a different location, and he's the only one who was returned."

"Maybe he wasn't up to standards, and the aliens pressed the reject button."

I could easily see this happening.

My parents' dining room table normally seated six. Tonight, it had been expanded to seat nine plus a high chair. It was a small house with a small dining room that now had wall-to-wall table.

"It's six o'clock," my father said. "They're late. They're always late."

The front door crashed open, and the girls rushed in. Angie the grade A student, Mary Alice who thought she was a horse, and two-year-old Lisa. Baby Bert was in a sling contraption that draped around Valerie's shoulder.

"Lisa made poo-poo in her pants," Mary Alice said. "She's stinky."

"That's not an acceptable thing to say," Valerie said. "'Stinky' is a hurtful adjective."

"Well, she don't smell like roses," Grandma said. "I'm pretty sure she's stinky."

My father was already at his seat at the head of the table. "Where's my ham? It's after six."

Albert Kloughn, Valerie's husband and the father of two of her four kids, came in last with his arms filled with presents and the diaper bag slung over his shoulder. Kloughn is my height, has thinning sandy-colored hair, a face like a cherub, and a body like the Pillsbury Doughboy. He's sweet but clueless. This is an especially bad combination for him, since he's a lawyer.

My sister Valerie was the perfect child all through school. Her long hair was sleek and blond. Her grades were excellent. She was never caught smoking or sneaking out her bedroom window. And she actually liked to attend mass. I was the problem child. I broke my arm trying to fly off the garage roof, smoked my first and last joint at Girl Scout camp, and I could see no point in learning to multiply and divide when I had a calculator that did it for me.

Valerie's hair is still sleek and blond, and so far, no one's caught her smoking. Her perfection was slightly marred when she divorced her philandering first husband, but she's still one up on me because she's remarried now, and has given my mother grandchildren. The closest I come to grandchildren for my mother is a hamster.

Grandma took Lisa to the bathroom for cleanup, and everyone else worked at squeezing themselves around the table. I helped my mother bring the food out. Virginia-baked ham, red gravy, mashed potatoes, green beans, applesauce, and macaroni salad.

Angie took a small portion of everything, and Mary Alice

sat with her arms crossed over her chest. “There’s no hay,” she said. “What am I supposed to eat? Horses eat hay.”

“You’re not a horse,” Grandma said, sitting Lisa in the high chair. “Have some ham.”

“I don’t like ham,” Mary Alice said. “I like hay.”

Grandma looked at Valerie. “Are you feeding this child hay?”

“Of course not,” Valerie said. “She has a wonderful imagination.”

“Well, she better imagine she likes ham or she’s not getting birthday cake,” Grandma said.

“Albert and I don’t threaten the children with punishment when they’re simply expressing their preferences,” Valerie said. “We try to show them alternative solutions.” Valerie turned to Mary Alice. “You could pretend that the ham is hay. Wouldn’t that be fun?”

Mary Alice kept her arms crossed and looked at Valerie like she had corn growing out of her ears.

My father had ham and potatoes and macaroni piled on his plate. “Gravy!” he said.

Morelli passed the gravy, and my mother joined us at the table. She had a tumbler of dark amber liquid that she passed off as iced tea, but we all knew was whiskey. She was in survival mode.

Lisa had been given mashed potatoes, small pieces of ham, and applesauce. She dumped it all onto her high chair tray and smeared it around. She threw her spoon across the table, and mashed a handful of glop into her hair.

Valerie smiled serenely at Lisa, and it occurred to me that Valerie's mood might be helped along by some form of controlled substance now that she was no longer breastfeeding.

Morelli had his arm draped across the back of my chair. He was calmly sipping wine and smiling. This was low stress for him. His family was even crazier than mine. His brother has been divorced twice and married three times. All to the same woman. They have so many kids I lost count. And that's just the tip of the Morelli family iceberg. His Grandma Bella dresses in black like she's an extra in a Sicilian mob movie, and she gives people *the eye*. If you annoy her you run the risk of getting boils and having your hair fall out. Stan Malinowski said Bella gave him the eye, and he had penis shrinkage.

Kloughn was wearing his lawyer uniform of chinos, a wrinkled white dress shirt, and a red and blue striped tie. He poured red gravy over his ham and potatoes, leaned across the table to get the salt, and the tip of his tie dragged across the gravy. He dabbed at his tie with his napkin.

"No problem," Kloughn said. "Valerie buys my ties on the cheap off the Internet, don't you, cuddleumpkins? They look just like real ties except they're made in China and you don't want to get too close to a flame."

My mother slurped down iced tea, and Valerie poured herself a glass of wine. My father had his head down, shoveling in ham.

"What's going on with the shoe snatcher?" Grandma asked Morelli. "Any new developments?"

"No new developments," Morelli said.

"Are you talking about the deli manager disappearances?" Kloughn asked. "Do you know what people are saying? They're saying it's aliens."

"That's what I figured!" Grandma said. "They're beaming up managers. Probably need them for some intergalactic resort."

"I never met the man who owns the deli," Kloughn said, "but I represented his Aunt Sissy in a lawsuit. If you ask me the whole family is screwy."

"Did you win the case?" Grandma asked.

"Not exactly," Kloughn said. "Sissy drove off a bridge on her way to my office one day and killed herself. I think it was accidental, but I guess there's no way to know for sure. She might have had a few drinky-poos before getting behind the wheel." Kloughn tucked his tie into his shirt and carefully cut his ham. "She was ninety-three when she died."

"Imagine that," Grandma said. "Only ninety-three."

The ham was dripping with gravy, and Kloughn leaned close to his plate to eat. "She had a lot of things to say about her nephew, Ernie. She said he was a weird kid, like he wanted to be emperor of the universe. Personally, I don't think that's so weird. I mean, lots of people want to be emperor of the universe, right? Anyway, I guess he always had a lot of schemes going while he was on his path to world domination. Sissy said he would always do anything to make money. When he was in seventh grade he sold his little sister to one of his classmates."

"How did that work out?" Morelli asked.

"Sissy didn't say," Kloughn said, "but I know they aren't on good terms. He might have tried to sell her a second time in high school. And he had aspirations of being a movie star. He has a bunch of movies he made on YouTube."

"Real movies?" Grandma asked.

"They're like homemade movies," Kloughn said. "Some of them are a little s-e-x-y."

"Daddy watches sexy movies," Angie said to her mother. "Is he a perv?"

"No," Valerie said. "He's a Taurus."

When we were done eating, I helped my mom clear the dishes. We brought the cake to the table, sang "Happy Birthday" to Valerie, and she opened her presents. I was the only one to give her a BeDazzler kit.

I ate two pieces of cake and pushed back from the table, debating whether I should return to the Snake Pit to take another shot at capturing Waggle. If I didn't get him tonight it would be a week before I'd get another chance. Truth is, a lot could happen in a week. Waggle could get beamed up by the shoe aliens. He could choke on a chicken bone. He could become a Buddhist monk and move to Nepal. All these possibilities sounded good to me.

The party was over at eight o'clock. Valerie rounded up her kids and went home, and Morelli drove me back to the deli.

"What's the plan for the rest of the night?" Morelli asked. "Do you want me to hang around while you lock up?"

"No. Not necessary. You can go home, and I'll have Hal drive me to your house when I'm done here."

He kissed me, told me to be careful, and waited until I was inside the deli before he pulled away.

Only two customers were still lingering in a booth when I walked in. Stretch was busy cleaning his station, and Lula was taking inventory for the purveyor orders. Raymond was squatting down behind the counter, sneaking a smoke. I didn't see Hal.

"Where's Hal?" I asked.

"He took out the trash," Lula said.

"How long ago?"

"Not that long. Maybe ten minutes."

"Have you checked on him?"

"No one's gonna beam up Hal. He's the size of a rhino."

I went to the register, looked at the monitor, and went breathless.

"There's something on the ground by the dumpster," I said. "Tell me it's not a shoe."

Lula looked at the monitor. "It could just be a piece of garbage," she said. "Sometimes garbage could look like a shoe."

Lula, Dalia, and I went to the back door and stared out into the parking area. No Hal. A large black running shoe was beside the dumpster.

"Hal," Lula yelled. "Come on out and quit joking on us. This isn't funny."

Silence.

"This is freaky," Lula said. "Hal isn't even the manager."

I went to the monitor and used the rewind function to scroll back. I stopped the rewind when I saw Hal walk out the back door with a bag of garbage. He went to the dumpster, tossed the bag in, and turned toward the back door. He paused and looked left. Something obviously had captured his attention. He crossed the lot to investigate and moved off the screen. Time passed. Hard to say if it was a single heartbeat or ten minutes. I couldn't drag my eyes away, and I couldn't breathe. And then suddenly a shoe sailed into view from the left side of the lot and landed by the dumpster.

"Holy crap," Lula said. "Holy hell. Holy moly."

I saw car lights flash in front of the deli. I hit the real-time button on the remote and saw two Rangeman cars pull up and park in the back alley.

Ranger was the first one through the front door. He was followed by two more Rangeman patrolmen.

"Is anyone missing other than Hal?" Ranger asked. "We saw him go off the screen and he's not responding."

"No," I said. "Just Hal. No one was watching the monitor when it happened. We realized he was missing, and I hit rewind. We saw the shoe come over, and then you arrived."

I followed Ranger to the back lot. Kan Kleen Dry Cleaners was next door to the deli. It was a storefront operation that sent clothes off-site for cleaning. Doors were shuttered at seven o'clock. The lot was used for pickup and delivery and employee parking. It was currently empty of vehicles. A small dumpster sat to one side. A private home was next in the lineup. It had a high brick wall enclosing its small backyard. Narrow alleys ran between all the buildings on the street.

Ranger's men were setting up extra lights and crime scene tape.

"Did you call the police?" I asked Ranger.

"No. I want to comb the scene before they contaminate it. I'll bring them in when we're done here. Keep everyone inside until I talk to them, and put the CLOSED sign on the door."

"This is getting old," Dalia said. "Bad enough all the managers disappeared, now it's anyone who goes out the back door. And every time someone goes missing we have to hang around until the police dismiss us. I'm done. I'm out of here. I quit."

"I would quit as well," Raymond said, "but I am unfortunately needing my paycheck. I have debts that will be painful to my person if I fall behind."

I looked over at Stretch. He was slumped in a corner booth, nodding off.

"He will stay," Raymond said. "He gets nicky-nacky from the lady who works in the cleaning establishment next door. It's not so easy to get good nicky-nacky on a regular basis."

I was afraid to ask what constituted good nicky-nacky, so I just nodded my head in agreement. At least neither of them were quitting.

"I'm feeling stressed," Lula said. "I'm worried about Hal. I'm beginning to doubt my theory about space aliens. It's one thing to beam people up for experimental probing and then return them to earth. This feels different. This feels more like there's a maniac out there. And I'm not in favor of maniacs."

I wasn't in favor of maniacs either, and I had a sick stomach. Three people associated with me were missing. I felt like two were directly my bad. Wayne Kulicki and Hal wouldn't have been in harm's way if it wasn't for me. I felt especially sick over Hal. He was a good person, and he'd been abducted while trying to protect me.

"The worst part is now that it might not be aliens, we don't know what's happening to these people," Lula said. "I don't even want to think about it. They could be . . . you know."

"Dead," Raymond said. "I fear someone is doing a very bad thing."

I went to the back door and stood next to Ranger. His men were systematically inching along the blacktopped parking area next to the deli, looking for clues.

"Did you find anything?" I asked him.

"No. The cameras scan to the dry cleaner's dumpster. Hal walked past the dumpster and out of camera range. He obviously thought the situation was benign. He didn't have his gun drawn. He didn't look concerned. We haven't found any signs of struggle. No blood. No torn clothing."

"Have you seen the latest medical report on Vinnie?"

"The one that suggested he might have been shot with a tranq dart? Yes, I have that report. It would explain the lack of evidence showing there was a struggle."

"What about Hal's shoe?"

"We haven't touched the shoe. CSI will test the shoe, but I'd be surprised if they find anything. Shoes from previous victims haven't been helpful."

I told him about my conversation with Wulf.

"I heard he was in town," Ranger said. "Hard to believe he's investigating the disappearances. I'd be more inclined to believe he's responsible for them."

"Where do you go from here?"

"I use my resources to find the missing people. And I go proactive."

"What does that mean?" I asked him. "How can you go proactive?"

"I can take Hal's place."

"Omigod. You're going to work here, making sandwiches?"

Ranger backed me into the wall and leaned into me. "You think I can't make sandwiches?"

"I've never seen you make a sandwich."

"You've seen me do other things. Have you ever seen me do anything badly?"

He had the hint of a smile curling at the corners of his mouth, and his eyes were dark. This wasn't a display of ego. This was foreplay, and it went straight to my doodah. I had a rush of heat erupt in my chest and head south. I'd been intimate with Ranger, and it wasn't an experience easily forgotten. It wasn't an experience any woman would *want* to forget.

"Who's going to run Rangeman if you're in the deli full-time?"

"I can run Rangeman off-site."

"Hal had other responsibilities besides making sandwiches."

"Hal was here to keep you safe," Ranger said.

"And now you're going to keep me safe?"

"Full-time."

"Morelli isn't going to like this."

"I'll hand you over to him when we close at night, and I'll expect you back in the morning. If you aren't with Morelli, you're with me."

Truth is, I didn't mind the arrangement. I wasn't exactly Rambo. And I didn't want to be the next victim with one shoe on and one shoe off.

Two Trenton PD patrol cars arrived five minutes after Ranger made the phone call to report Hal missing. Jimmy Krut showed up ten minutes later. Morelli was a couple minutes behind Krut. I'd made the call to Morelli.

I stayed close to the building, in front of the open back door. Morelli and Ranger were standing toe to toe beyond the dumpster. Morelli was hands on hips, his cop face firmly in place. Focused. Alpha dog posture. Ranger had his back to me. His arms were relaxed at his side, but his stance was solid, shoulders back from years in the military. Ranger was alpha dog times two. There was professional respect on both sides. And there was personal distrust simmering below the surface.

Morelli cut his eyes to me, his gaze held for a couple beats, and his attention returned to Ranger. They were talking about me. Their intentions were probably good, but I felt like I was being auctioned off on eBay.

"Hey!" I yelled. "Do you want to include me in this conversation?"

"No," Morelli said.

I couldn't see Ranger's face, but I knew that got a smile from him. I did a massive eye roll, called them idiots, and retreated into the deli, slamming the door behind me.

"You look like you need pie," Lula said.

I looked around the room. It was empty.

"Where is everyone?" I asked.

"Dalia quit. She said if anyone wants to talk to her they can kiss her ass and good luck finding her. She said she was going to get into her car and start driving west and not stop until she hit the Pacific Ocean. Raymond and Stretch went home. They said unless you were gonna start paying overtime they weren't staying late no more."

"What kind of pie do we have?"

"Apple, coconut custard, lemon meringue but I wouldn't recommend it, and chocolate pudding pie."

"What's wrong with the lemon meringue?"

"It smells like cat pee," Lula said.

I went to the fridge and pulled out a chocolate pudding pie and extra whipped cream.

"Bring two forks," Lula said.

We dug into the pie, and I looked over at Lula.

"What's going on here? What's the motive? What's with the shoe?"

"Maniacs don't always have motives," Lula said. "At least none that make sense. Like maybe the devil told someone to snatch people and leave a shoe behind."

"Suppose it wasn't the devil. Suppose it was someone more normal. Why would someone want to take people associated with the management of the deli?"

"That's a tough one," Lula said. "And why did they snatch Hal? He wasn't a manager."

"Maybe Hal was a mistake."

"Okay, so who would benefit from having bad things happening at the deli?" Lula asked. "There's Ernie Sitz, but he's supposed to be on the moon or something. I don't see how this would do him any good. Except maybe he would be looking for revenge. Like if he couldn't have the deli then no one could have it."

"If that was the motive he could just torch it."

"Yeah, but that wouldn't be as much fun," Lula said.

I hadn't thought of this in terms of fun, but I suppose it was as good a motive as any.

"What about the bodies?" I asked. "Where are they?"

"That's got about a million answers," Lula said. "They could be on a hook in the deep freeze of a butcher shop. Or they could be in a shallow grave in the Pine Barrens. Or they could be still alive and chained up in someone's cellar. I don't think they got thrown in the Delaware, because one of them would have floated up by now."

I didn't like any of those answers. I put my head down and forked into the pie.

One of the Rangeman guys took Lula home. I went home with Morelli. Bob danced around us when we entered. Morelli ruffled Bob's ears and locked the door.

"Now what?" he asked. "Television? Glass of wine? Frozen waffle? Bed?"

"Bed. I just worked my way through half a pudding pie, and I'm done."

"Only half a pie?"

"Lula ate the other half."

"Works for me. Bed was my choice too."

"What do you think happened to Hal?"

"I don't know. He's a big guy. He's strong. He was wearing a sidearm. Whatever happened to him was unexpected. He didn't feel threatened when he walked out of camera range. It was as if he was going to see someone he knew or someone who couldn't possibly harm him. The shoe was thrown in three minutes later. It was a fast takedown."

"Tranquilizer dart?"

"It's a possibility," Morelli said.

"Do you think I'm going to be the next one to disappear?"

"No. I'm more worried about Ranger than I am about the manager snatcher."

With good reason, I thought.

# CHAPTER THIRTEEN

I HEARD MORELLI moving around the room in the dark. He was getting dressed. I looked at the clock. Five-thirty Saturday morning. He was right on schedule, even though it was a Saturday. Thank God it wasn't my schedule. I rolled over and snuggled under the quilt.

"Don't roll over," he said. "You have to get up."

"It's too early," I said. "I don't get up before the sun."

The bedroom light flashed on.

"That was yesterday," Morelli said, throwing my clothes onto the bed. "You have to leave with me today. I'm dropping you off at Rangeman on my way to work."

I squinted at him, my eyes not totally adjusted to the light. "What? Why? Are you serious?"

"It's the deal we made. You're either with me or with Ranger."

"Not at five-thirty in the morning!"

"At all hours of the morning. You set yourself up to be a walking target. I get why you did it. But it was a stupid idea."

"It seemed smart when I thought of it."

He flipped the quilt off me and pulled me out of bed. "You're such a cupcake."

I pushed my hair out of my face and tried to wake up. "I need coffee."

Morelli grinned at me. "You don't have any clothes on."

"It's all your fault."

"Yeah, I remember." He settled his hands at my waist and drew me closer. "Maybe no one would notice if I was ten minutes late this morning."

"I need more than ten minutes."

"I don't," Morelli said.

It was almost seven o'clock when Morelli turned me over to the armed guard at the front desk of Rangeman. I took the elevator to the fifth-floor control room and made my way to Ranger's office.

The office was small. A desk and two chairs. A bank of monitors on one wall. No window. Private half bath. No artwork. No photos of family. Walls were white. Chairs were black leather. A MacBook Pro was open on a glass and ebony desk. Ranger was wearing the standard Rangeman uniform of black cargo pants and black long-sleeved, collared shirt with the Rangeman logo on the sleeve. He stood and came over to me when I entered.

"Have you had breakfast?" he asked.

I nodded yes. I'd had a frozen waffle and coffee.

"I could use more coffee," I said.

"I have morning meetings," Ranger said. "I'll be done around nine-thirty."

"I'm supposed to unlock the deli at ten."

"No problem. You can hang in my apartment until I'm done here. There's coffee in the kitchen."

My apartment is utilitarian with secondhand furniture and a bathroom that dates back to the fifties. The best I can say is that I try to keep it neat. Morelli's house is a man cave with a toaster and a dog. My parents' house looks like the set from *All in the Family.*

Ranger's apartment was worthy of *Architectural Digest.* Small, ultramodern, well-equipped kitchen. Eating nook off the kitchen. The living room was furnished with a few sleek, comfortable pieces. An office that also served as a den, with a two-seater couch and a flat-screen television, was attached to the single bedroom. The bedroom was dark and cool and masculine. King-size bed with expensive linens. A dressing room where his housekeeper had all his clothes neatly pressed and folded. A high-gloss bathroom that always had the scent of Bulgari Green shower gel escaping from the walk-in shower.

Hanging in Ranger's apartment wasn't a hardship. I took the

elevator to his floor, let myself in, and went to the kitchen. I helped myself to coffee and looked around. Fresh fruit in a bowl next to an airtight glass container of walnuts and almonds. No donuts. Ranger ate healthy.

I wouldn't mind going back to bed, but I didn't want to send Ranger the wrong message, so I stayed in the living room and checked my email. I texted Lula I'd meet her at the deli at ten o'clock.

Ranger came to collect me at nine forty-five. He exchanged his Rangeman shirt for a plain black T-shirt, grabbed a handful of nuts from the jar on the kitchen counter, and we left his apartment.

Stretch, Raymond, and Lula were on the sidewalk in front of the deli when Ranger and I pulled up in his black Porsche Cayenne Turbo.

"What's the drill?" Ranger asked me.

"I open the door for Raymond and Stretch, and they get the deli ready for the lunch crowd. They get the fry station up and running. They do all the food prep."

"Does any of this involve going into the back by the dumpster?"

"There are a bunch of vendors who deliver to the back door. Laundry, the butcher, Central GP. They all show up before the deli opens for business. One of us goes out and gets the stuff and brings it in and puts it away."

"What's your role besides opening the front door?"

"I fill in wherever I'm needed. Sometimes I help make sandwiches. Sometimes I answer the phone. When Hal was here it gave me a chance to step back and watch the customers."

"Anyone of interest?"

"Not really. One regular caught my attention, but I think he's probably just a guy who lives in the neighborhood and doesn't like to cook."

Ranger and I got out of the Porsche, I unlocked the door, and we all went in and looked around. Everything seemed to be okay. No dead bodies. No extra shoes. No sneakers-up rats or cockroaches. Ranger went to the back door and stepped out. I followed behind him. It was eerily quiet with no sign of Hal. My vision blurred, and I felt like someone was squeezing my heart.

Ranger pulled the yellow crime scene tape down and threw it in the dumpster. He wrapped an arm around me and kissed me on my forehead. "We'll find him," he said.

The Central GP truck rumbled down the back alley and swung into the deli's parking area. Frankie got out from behind the wheel and handed me the itemized bill.

"You're early," I said.

"Yeah, it's a light day. Didn't take me as long to load the truck. Tell the boys I had to short them on the powdered sugar, but I'll make up for it on Monday."

Ranger and I put the groceries away, and I told Stretch about the powdered sugar, which I suspected was drug code.

"What's up for the morning?" Lula asked me. "We only got one bad guy to look for, and we don't know where to find him."

"Steph's coming with me," Ranger said. "We're going for a walk."

The area around the deli was mixed. There were gentrified pockets, but for the most part, the buildings were neglected, housing marginally legal businesses and a struggling population of dysfunctional, fractured families with gangbanger kids.

We started our walk in the alley and methodically canvassed the neighborhood. We walked slowly, listening and looking for anything out of the ordinary.

"You think the kidnapper is local," I said.

"I think there's a local connection."

It was almost noon when we returned to the deli.

"What do you think?" I asked Ranger. "Did you see anything interesting?"

"The police have already questioned everyone in a four-block grid. They came up with nothing, but I wanted to see for myself."

"And?"

"Two buildings have vans parked in the alley. And there were four garages that were closed and locked. I'll have someone check them out."

"You think they packed Hal off in a van?"

"No stone unturned," Ranger said. "They immediately disabled his cellphone, so we weren't able to track him."

"You didn't have a GPS gizmo sewn onto the hem of his shirt?"

"We tried that but they kept getting mangled in the laundry."

I was being sarcastic. Ranger might have been serious.

"These kidnappings are well planned and well executed," Ranger said. "The victim is quickly removed with little forensic evidence left behind. And so far, no one has stepped forward asking for ransom. No one is bragging on social media. No bodies have been found."

"Except for Vinnie."

"Vinnie is an anomaly," Ranger said.

"Wow, 'anomaly.' That's a big word."

The barest hint of a smile twitched at the corners of Ranger's mouth. "I know a few."

Lula threw her hands up when she saw us. "It's about time you came back. We got a situation here. We just opened and the place is packed and there's a line out the front door. That stupid television station ran another special on this place. All about the people getting beamed up and leaving a shoe behind. And it was about me and Hal and how we were connected somehow. And how we were a sight to see. I don't even know what that means. It might not be flattering in the way they said it. And if that isn't bad enough, we haven't got a waitress. Who's gonna wait tables? I'm telling you it's chaos."

"You wait tables," I said. "I'll do the sandwiches and Ranger can take the phones."

"Good luck with that," Lula said. "The phones won't stop ringing."

"I have my fry oil ready," Raymond said. "Let's do this."

Lula was wearing a royal blue bandage dress that was so tight it looked like it was painted on her. It had short sleeves and a low scoop neck that barely contained her massive breasts. The skirt wrapped around her Kardashian butt and hung two inches below her hoo-ha. She sashayed out on five-inch stilettos and distributed menus. She dropped one, bent at the waist to pick it up, and the bandage dress skirt did nothing to hide the full moon. Only a hint of her red thong was visible, the rest being sucked up into the Grand Canyon of Voluptuousness.

There was a collective gasp from the dining room.

"I must now pour bleach into my eyes," Raymond said. "We are lucky the morality police don't have jurisdiction in Trenton. They would beat her with a stick many times."

"New plan," Ranger said to me. "You wait tables and we'll put Lula on sandwiches."

"No one's going to eat a sandwich she makes after seeing this," Stretch said. "Give her phones and takeout."

I handed Ranger a menu. "You're up for sandwiches. Raymond works the fry station and Stretch plates and nukes. Everything you need to know is on this gravy-stained menu. Your workstation is behind Stretch."

Ranger eyed the workstation. "Got it," he said.

I tapped Lula on the shoulder and told her we had a new plan. "We think you'd be better behind the counter."

"I'm good behind the counter, but it seems a shame people can't appreciate my new dress when I'm hidden back there." Lula looked down at herself. "This here's a bitchin' dress."

"True, but it turns out there's not enough of it for waiting tables. When you bend over all your secrets are on display."

"Well, anyone would be lucky to see my secrets."

"Maybe for dessert," I said, "but not before lunch."

"I guess you got a point."

I took the order pad and went to the first table. I was wearing jeans and a girlie pink V-neck T-shirt and sneakers. No secrets were exposed.

It was an easy order. One number sixteen. One number seven with cheese fries. One number seven with onion rings. I stuck the order on the spindle on the service bar in front of Stretch and yelled out the order. We didn't have computers or iPads or any of that tech stuff. We were old school. I imagine it works great if you have people who know what they're doing and aren't dopers. At the Red River Deli it was hit-or-miss.

The second table wanted egg salad, but it had to be on a croissant, hold the pickle, a turkey club on gluten-free, no third slice of bread, and a corned beef with the works. I handed it in and hoped Ranger knew how to do *the works*.

At three o'clock we were still serving lunch.

"I am out of my freshly cut frozen French fries," Raymond said. "I cannot go on. You must lock the door and not let anyone else in."

"Now see, that's a brilliant idea," Lula said. "I'm not answering any more phones, either. Some of these calls I'm taking aren't about food. I've had people calling in making inappropriate comments about my mooning incident today."

"Someone has put it on social media," Raymond said. "I have seen it. The picture is truly terrible, but you have three thousand likes. I do not even want to come to work tomorrow. I fear it will be hell."

"I find this inspiring, now that I know I'm a sensation again," Lula said. "I've got an idea for a new creation. I'm going to call it the Lula Moonwich."

Ranger had been making sandwiches for hours. He didn't have a speck of mayo, mustard, or ketchup on him. His station was immaculate. Every sandwich had been perfect and cut with precision.

"Impressive," I said.

He smiled. "I have good knife skills."

I hung the CLOSED sign on the front door, and the dining room was empty twenty minutes later.

Ranger was hands on hips. "What happens now?"

"I chipped a nail answering phones," Lula said. "It was my best nail too. It was the one with the stars-and-stripes decal. I'm going to have it repaired before we start with the dinner people. I gotta look my best in case the television crew comes back."

"We can turn the door sign around at five o'clock," Stretch said. "That'll give us an hour and a half to reorganize. Someone has to make a store run. We've never done this many covers before. We're out of everything."

"I'll make the store run," I said. "Give me a list."

# CHAPTER FOURTEEN

RANGER STOOD BY the shopping cart while I threw bags of bread and rolls into it.

"Have you checked with your office?" I asked him. "Do you have any leads on Hal?"

"Nothing I'd call a lead, but it's early. Right now, we're gathering information from a lot of different sources."

"Legally?"

"Sometimes."

Ranger employed a bunch of ex-cons who had extraordinary skills. Hackers, pickpockets, second-story experts, locksmiths, and safecrackers. His clients were kept safe by men who knew how the bad guys operated and knew how to stop them. These men also had contacts who could be useful at retrieving stolen property and missing deli managers.

"The rye bread feels stale," I said. "Do you think I should pass on it?"

"I think it doesn't matter if it's stale as long as it's not covered in blue mold. The people who are standing in line to get into the deli aren't interested in the food. They're there for the freak show."

This was true. The deli had turned into a freak show. Workers disappeared without a trace. Weird sandwiches came out of the kitchen. Customers got mooned by the waitress. And the result of the freak show was a packed deli.

"Harry must have mixed emotions about the deli," I said. "He took possession of it and instantly started having problems. On the other hand, the problems seem to be making the deli a huge success."

"I doubt Harry would be bothered by any of those problems," Ranger said. "He's made his share of people disappear in the past. The only difference is that most of those people were found shortly after they were shot, choked, or bludgeoned with a shovel."

We moved from the bread aisle to frozen foods and filled a second cart with French fries and onion rings.

"I'm seeing a whole new side of you," I said to Ranger. "Who would have thought you'd be so at home making sandwiches and shopping for food?"

"Domestic Ranger."

"Exactly. You're going to make some lucky lady a wonderful husband someday."

He wrapped an arm around me and pulled me close. "I have other marital skills. Would you like to see them?"

"Not in the frozen food section."

Ranger grinned. "Name the place."

"I'll give it some thought."

"You're playing with me," Ranger said.

"And you?"

"I'm not playing."

When I'm this close to Ranger, and his lips are brushing against my ear, it's difficult to think beyond the desire to rip his clothes off. Fortunately, we were in a supermarket, and by the time we got to the car I would have my mind redirected to other activities . . . like finding Hal.

We added jars of pickles and sauerkraut to the cart and checked out.

"Maybe you should add extra cameras to the deli," I said to Ranger.

He loaded the groceries into the back of the SUV. "I don't want to make another kidnapping seem impossible. Our best shot is still for them to go after you or me."

"You're sure you can find me, right?"

He looked down at my shoes. "Your shoes are equipped with locators. Both of them."

"When did that happen?"

"Right after you bought them. About a month ago."

A couple years ago I would have been incensed and outraged. This afternoon I was resigned. I had no control over Ranger.

"What if I don't get to keep a shoe?" I asked him.

"Glad you asked. I have a miniaturized transponder I'd like to implant."

"*Implant*? Where?"

"You get to choose. I get to assist," Ranger said.

"No, no, no. No way. No how."

"It's small. You won't know you're carrying it."

"How do I get it out?"

"There's a string attached."

I felt myself go slack-jawed and bug-eyed for a moment. "Seriously?"

"Hal was wearing a tracking device attached to his belt. We began chasing the tracker down minutes after Hal disappeared. We found it two blocks from the deli. It was in a dumpster along with the rest of his clothes. He didn't have a tracking device in his shoe, so we don't know if he was allowed to keep it. Having the transponder buried inside you is the best way I know to keep you safe."

"Morelli almost had a cow when you taped a wire to me. How am I going to explain this?"

"You can begin by telling him it was the best twenty minutes of your short life."

"Twenty minutes?"

"I could do the job in less time, but it wouldn't be as memorable," Ranger said.

"It's tempting, but I think I'm going to stick with the shoe."

"You could also swallow the transponder."

"What if it gets stuck somewhere?"

"It's unlikely that it would get stuck, but you would check to make sure it leaves your body."

"Eeuuww."

"Babe," Ranger said.

It was almost five o'clock when we carried everything into the deli. Raymond and Stretch were at their stations doing prep work. Ranger's housekeeper, Ella, was at the sandwich station.

I looked over at Ranger. "You brought Ella in to make sandwiches."

"I can't watch the customers if I'm making sandwiches," Ranger said. "And at some point, we're going to have to send you out to the dumpster while I'm watching the monitor."

Oh crap. The suicide mission. If it went wrong, I'd be stripped naked, written on with a marker pen, and I couldn't even imagine what happened next.

"Are you sure you'll be able to get to me in time if you're watching in here?" I asked him.

"I have men doing undercover surveillance from the building behind the deli. And I have men on constant patrol, circling the block, in unmarked cars."

"And the instant someone lays a hand on me all hell will break loose, right?"

"Wrong," Ranger said. "We want them to lead us to the other captives."

Double crap. I really hated the strip-naked part, and I feared it happening sooner rather than later.

"If you captured the kidnappers right away, you could *force* them to tell you about the rest of the stuff," I said.

"Are you sure you don't want to swallow the transponder?" Ranger asked.

"I'll think about it."

"Don't think too long," he said.

People were lining up outside the deli, and Lula pushed her way in through the front door.

"You're not going to believe what I just saw," she said. "I was coming back here from getting my nail repaired, and I was looking for a parking place. I was driving all over creation being that those idiot people waiting to get in here took up the parking places. Anyways, I went down one of the alleys and all of a sudden something black caught my eye. It was crawling out of a window on the third floor of a building. And then it stood up on the ledge, and I could see it was a man all dressed in black. And then he spread his arms out, and he had bat wings. And next thing he stepped off the ledge and flew away."

"He *flew* away?" I said.

"Well, it looked like he was flying because he had his bat wings out, but I guess you could say he was dropping."

"From the third floor?"

"Yeah, except he touched down on a little awning over a back door, and sort of swooped off to the ground. He folded his wings, turned and walked between two buildings and disappeared. I was a distance away, but I'm pretty sure it was Wulf."

"I don't suppose you could have mistaken a cape for bat wings," I said.

"I guess that's a possibility," Lula said.

"Where was the alley?" Ranger asked.

"It was one street over," Lula said. "The awning he landed on said 'KitKat.' It's a bar. I think there are apartments over it."

"Someone needs to turn the sign in the door and start letting people in," Stretch said. "It looks like it's getting ugly out there."

Three minutes later, every table was full, and there were ten people in line at the takeout counter. I was the only waitress, and customers were getting surly. The first food came up before I was done taking orders. I grabbed the plates and plunked them down on a table.

"This isn't our food," a woman said. "We ordered the number seven and ten."

I picked the plates up and turned to the room. "Who ordered whatever this is?"

Three tables claimed it. I looked over at Ranger and caught him smiling.

"Order up," Stretch said.

Crap! I gave the plates away and ran to get the new order.

By eight o'clock no one was smiling. Not me. Not Lula. Not Ranger. Not Stretch, Raymond, or Ella. And certainly not the customers. Turns out, I'm not the world's best waitress, and

Lula's patience gets thin after forty-five minutes of phone orders.

We shut down at nine o'clock. My feet were killing me and my brain was numb.

"I vote we discontinue phone orders," Lula said. "I'm underappreciated on the phone. I give these fools my happy sunshine voice and all they do is bark orders back at me. It's a demoralizing experience, and after a while I find myself getting phone rage and wanting to smash something. Toward the end I was thinking I got a gun in my handbag and I could kill the phone."

"It does not sound like a terrible idea," Raymond said. "I often feel just that way about my fries. Sometimes I leave them in the oil too long on purpose because I hate them. Kill the fuckers, I think to myself. Kill the fucking fries."

"Damn," Lula said. "Do you kill a *lot* of fries?"

"No," Raymond said. "After I kill just one or two I take a break and smoke a big doobie and I feel much better."

"I guess that's the difference between you professionals and us amateurs," Lula said. "You got good work habits established."

Ranger was holding a garbage bag. "Someone needs to take this to the dumpster," he said.

"I'd do it but I just got my nail repaired," Lula said. "I'm not taking no chances at getting it broken again."

"Pass me by," Stretch said.

"I would not do this if all of the earth was on fire with the exception of the parking lot," Raymond said. "I would not go out that back door. There is evil waiting in the darkness."

Ranger handed the bag over to me. "Showtime," he said. "Don't rush it. We want to give these guys a good shot at you. I don't know how many more days I can take working in this deli."

It took me a couple beats to process, and then it hit me. Ranger was sending me out to get kidnapped. Crap!

"Suppose they shoot me or stab me?" I said.

"That's not the way they work," Ranger said. "There's no evidence of violence."

"Suppose there's some other miscreant out there, and he wants to rob me?"

"I'm wearing an earbud, talking to my surveillance people," Ranger said. "They tell me there's no one in the area. Probably this is a dud night, but we'll try anyway."

"And if this miscreant comes along out of the blue and demands to take possession of our garbage, you should give it to him," Raymond said.

Ranger ordered everyone to stay behind in the kitchen, and I trudged to the back door with my garbage bag. Five minutes earlier I was stupefied tired. Now I was in adrenaline overload. My heart was beating hard, and my hand was sweaty on the doorknob. I opened the door and looked out. The small parking lot was well lit, but beyond it was blackness. Ranger's men were out there somewhere, and Ranger was watching on the monitor. It was all good, I told myself. I'd be fine.

I stepped out and moved toward the dumpster. I could hear the faint drone of traffic from the cross street. All else was quiet. I tried to pace myself, walking not too fast and not too slow. I tried to look natural. Just another day at the deli. I reached the dumpster and paused. Still no footsteps. No flying saucer hovering overhead. I heaved the garbage into the dumpster and turned. No one lurking behind me.

It's not over yet, I told myself. You still have to get back inside. I lingered for a moment so Ranger could see I was a brave soldier making an effort, and then I headed for the door.

I stepped in with a mix of emotions. Relief that nothing had happened, and disappointment that nothing had happened. Ranger closed and locked the door, slipped an arm around me, and my knees almost buckled.

"I'm okay," I said.

He kissed me on my forehead. "Babe."

"It says on the door that the deli opens at five o'clock on Sundays," Lula said. "Hallelujah. I need a break from this nuthouse."

"What about provisions?" I asked.

"No provisions on Sunday," Stretch said. "We should be okay. Sunday night is light."

"Saturday was also supposed to be light," Raymond said. "How did that turn out?"

I slumped in my seat in Ranger's Porsche. "I'm exhausted," I said. "I'm not waitress material. I'm glad this day is over."

"It's not over yet," Ranger said. "I'm curious about the Wulf window exit."

Ranger drove to the KitKat and parked one building away. It was an okay street. Mostly narrow, three-story residential row houses. Lots of graffiti but no gangbangers walking around shooting each other. There were lights on in the apartment above the bar. No lights on the third floor. The upstairs apartments were accessed through a door next to the bar. Ranger walked in, and I followed. We took the stairs to the third floor. There were two apartments up there. One facing front and one facing the rear.

Ranger knocked on the rear-facing apartment. No answer. The door was locked. Ranger took a pick from a pocket in his cargo pants and opened the door. We stood for a moment, letting our eyes adjust to the dark.

From what I could see it was an empty studio apartment. Small kitchenette on one side of the room. No furniture.

"It's empty," I said.

"Not empty," Ranger said. "Look in the corner."

"I can't see in the corner. You have better night vision than I do."

This was an understatement. Ranger had vision like a cat.

He flipped the light on, and I sucked in air. There were shoes in the corner. One of each kind. Ranger closed and locked the door behind us, and we walked to the corner with the shoes.

"There are two security cameras in here," Ranger said. "One over the door and one on the wall opposite the door."

"Infrared," I said. "I saw the red eye when we walked in."

Ranger went to the window. It was closed but not locked. He checked out the closet, the half fridge, the over-the-counter cabinets, and the bathroom.

"It's empty," he said. "I'm going to call it in to Trenton PD. The crime lab might be able to pick something up."

I was asleep on my feet when Morelli arrived twenty minutes later, ten minutes behind the two uniforms.

"Jimmy Krut has the flu," Morelli said. "I was next in the rotation. What's going on?"

Ranger told him Lula saw Wulf leave from the window, so we came to check things out after we closed the deli.

"And the door was unlocked and the unit empty?" Morelli asked.

"It was unlocked and empty," Ranger said.

This was true. Ranger had unlocked it.

"There are nine shoes," Ranger said. "We only know about six kidnappings."

Morelli looked happy to hear this. Truth is, Morelli loved his job. He wasn't happy about the blood and gore, but he loved the mystery. He loved the procedure. He loved solving the crime.

"The crime scene people are on their way," Morelli said. "Did you find anything interesting?"

"No," Ranger said. "It's clean. It's almost as if this was staged."

I was so tired I was swaying.

"I can't believe I'm saying this, but you're going to have to take her home with you," Morelli said to Ranger. "I'm going to be here for hours, and she's not going to last."

"No problem," Ranger said. "Let me know when you want her back."

Ranger's bedroom is cool and dark, dimly lit by ambient light coming from his office. His thousand-thread-count Egyptian cotton sheets are smooth and silky. His pillows are lump-free and perfect. The lightweight quilt is luxuriously soft. I was wearing panties and one of his T-shirts, and I was in my happy place. I was safe and secure in his bed. And I was alone. Ranger was in his office, catching up on work, recognizing that a romantic encounter with me at this time would be like making love to a dead person.

At some point during the night I woke up and felt Ranger next to me. He was warm, and there was the faint scent of his Bulgari Green shower gel. I fell back asleep, and when I woke up again it was morning, and he was gone.

# CHAPTER FIFTEEN

I SHOWERED AND dressed in clean clothes that Ella had left for me. A Rangeman black T-shirt and cargo pants that were in my size. There was hot coffee, fresh fruit, and croissants in the small kitchen. No sign of Ranger. When you own your own security business and live on the premises, every day is a work day.

Morelli called at nine-thirty to tell me he was in the lobby. I took the elevator down and texted Ranger that I was leaving.

"What's the plan for the day?" I asked when I was settled into Morelli's SUV.

"Grocery shopping. Pick up Grandma Bella and drop her off at the church for potluck brunch. She's bringing lasagna and a cake."

This sent a chill down my spine. Grandma Bella scared the heck out of me.

"Maybe you could leave me home when you get Bella," I said. "Give me a loaded gun and lock all the doors when you leave. I'll be fine."

"No."

"She scares me."

"She scares everybody," Morelli said. "It's her thing."

"Can we go out to lunch after we drop Bella off?"

"Yeah. As long as we're home in time for the game."

Shopping with Morelli is a whole different experience from shopping with Ranger. Morelli shops for a few staples for the week and for game food. Chips, dip, beer, M&M's, hot spicy wings, pepperoni pizza rolls.

"That's a lot of snacks," I said.

"Anthony, Big Wanger, and Mooch always come over for the Giants' game. It's tradition."

So here are some of the reasons I'm not married to Morelli. His job. His family. His friends. And the remaining reason is my inability to commit. The reason I'm not married to Ranger is much simpler. His life path doesn't include marriage. End of story.

We took the groceries back to Morelli's house, let Bob out to tinkle, and picked up Grandma Bella.

Grandma Bella squinted at me from the back seat. "What *she* doing here?" she said to Morelli.

"We're spending the afternoon together," Morelli said.

"You could do better," Bella said. "I don't like this one. I might give her the eye."

"You give her the eye, and I'll tell my mother on you."

"I'll give her the eye too."

"You can't give the eye to your daughter," Morelli said.

"I do what I want," Bella said.

Morelli was smiling. He thought this was amusing. He was the only one who was never threatened with the eye. He was Bella's favorite.

"What kind of cake are you bringing?" Morelli asked Bella.

"Chocolate. If you come to church you get some."

"I'll have to see how the day goes," Morelli said.

"You going to hell," Bella said. "You never go to church, and you got this slut in your car. Her grandma cheats at bingo. God don't like bingo cheats and sluts."

Morelli pulled up to the church and helped Bella into the building. She carried the cake, and he carried the fifteen-pound lasagna. He walked back to the car and got behind the wheel.

"That wasn't so bad," he said.

"She called me a slut."

"You made out better than I did. She said I was going to hell."

"Are you worried?" I asked him.

"Maybe a little," Morelli said. "Is Pino's okay for lunch?"

"Pino's is perfect. Were you able to learn anything from the apartment last night?"

"I don't have anything back from CSI," Morelli said. "There were a lot of prints. I'm sure some of them belonged to Ranger. I'll get a report on them today. The DNA stuff takes longer. The shoes were all men's. The apartment was rented to Robert Smith. The information on his rental form was bogus. All transactions were by mail. The owner of the building didn't care. He was happy to rent the unit. He collected six months' rent in advance."

"It's like these people are professional kidnappers. They plan ahead, and they don't leave any evidence behind."

"They leave evidence," Morelli said. "Everyone leaves evidence. We haven't found the evidence yet, but it's there."

"Were you able to find out who owned the security cameras?"

"They were placed after the unit was rented. We couldn't trace them. We shut them down but left them in place, so Ranger could send his tech over to take a look. His guy is better than my guy."

Big Wanger, Anthony, and Mooch were lined up on the couch, eyes glued to the television. Morelli was in the leather recliner. Bob was sitting next to Morelli, waiting for food to fall onto the floor. The coffee table was littered with takeout pizza boxes, empty beer cans, bowls of chips, and whatever.

"Do you want to sit?" Mooch asked me. "There's room on the couch."

"No, thanks," I said. "I just came in to gather up some of the trash. I don't want to encroach on your male-bonding experience."

"That happened in seventh grade," Big Wanger said. "We just tolerate each other now."

I put a bunch of empty beer cans in one of the empty pizza boxes and carted it all out to the kitchen. I stopped short at the kitchen door when I realized Wulf was lounging against the counter. He was wearing black slacks and a black cashmere sweater with the sleeves pushed up. No visible bat wings.

"We need to talk," Wulf said.

"Okay."

"As a courtesy to a friend, I'm looking for a man who is associated with the deli. I believe he's also involved in the kidnappings."

"Ernie Sitz? Harry the Hammer?"

"I'm not at liberty to say. I'm telling you this because I want you to persuade Ranger to remove his men from their surveillance positions. They're making my job difficult."

"You should talk to Ranger directly."

Wulf's mouth curved into a smile, but his eyes were cold. "Ranger and I have an adversarial history."

"I'll pass the message along, but I can't guarantee he'll listen to me."

"Understood."

"What were you doing in the apartment above the KitKat?"

"Tracking my prey."

"You left through the window," I said.

"There were people in the hall, fumbling for their apartment key. It seemed expedient to exit directly to the alley."

"The shoes?"

"The shoes are a mystery," Wulf said. He looked toward the living room. "I have to leave."

"Are you going to do the smoke thing?"

This time the smile was genuine. "Would you like me to do the smoke thing?"

"Yes."

*BANG!* Smoke swirled around Wulf, and he was gone.

Ranger picked me up in his sporty Porsche 911 Turbo at four o'clock. No Ella scrunched into the back seat.

"Where's Ella?" I asked.

"Tank is bringing her over. He's taking a shift on deli patrol tonight."

Tank is second-in-command at Rangeman. He's the guy who watches Ranger's back. He's a year younger than Ranger. He's twice Ranger's size. There's good reason he's called Tank.

"Do you think the deli patrol is necessary? Hard to believe the kidnappers would try to snatch someone after their apartment has been discovered."

Ranger drove away from Morelli's house and turned onto Hamilton Avenue. "There are problems with the apartment. These kidnappings are professionally executed. Very little forensic evidence is left behind. No time is wasted. Someone who meticulously planned out these crimes wouldn't have chosen a third-floor walk-up to play a role in the abduction. If the victims are unconscious, someone has to carry them up three flights of stairs. Not easy with someone like Hal. If they're conscious you have to walk them up the stairs at gunpoint. Too conspicuous. And then there are the shoes. Neatly piled in a corner of the otherwise empty apartment. They were purposely brought there. And there were more shoes than known kidnap victims."

"You think they were staged."

"The better question is *why* were they staged?"

This is why Ranger has his own security firm, and I'm barely able to pay my rent. He's observant. He connects the dots. He knows how to use his unique talents. I'm sure I have unique talents, but they haven't surfaced yet.

"Morelli said he asked you to send your tech over to check out the security cameras."

"The apartment didn't have an alarm system, so the cameras were strictly for surveillance. They had the ability to record and send to a separate location."

"Do you know the location? Were you able to see what it recorded?"

"The record function wasn't active. The cameras were sending to a location that's since been shut down. Sometimes we can still find the location, but not in this case."

"I had a surprise visit from Wulf this afternoon," I said. "He told me he was doing a favor for a friend, tracking down a man who was associated with the deli. He said you were making his job more difficult with your surveillance people."

“And he asked you to pass this on to me?”

“Yes. He said you had an adversarial history with him.”

“We’ve crossed paths,” Ranger said.

“Are you going to pull back on the surveillance?”

“No.”

“Am I taking the garbage out tonight?”

“No. I’m taking it out tonight,” Ranger said.

He pulled up to the deli. A Rangeman guy came out of the shadows and took Ranger’s place behind the wheel.

“Valet parking?” I said to Ranger.

“Sometimes it’s good to be me,” Ranger said.

It was Sunday, and the area around the train station was quiet. There was only sporadic traffic on the road in front of the deli, and no pedestrian traffic. Raymond and Stretch weren’t waiting at the door, and I had a stab of panic that they weren’t going to show up for work.

I unlocked the deli, and Ranger and I went in. The room smelled like fry grease and dill pickle and felt lonely without Raymond and Stretch.

“Do you hear that?” I asked Ranger. “There’s something making scratching sounds.”

“Mice in the walls,” Ranger said. “You can’t hear them when the fan is going over the fry station.”

“This place should be demolished.”

“Not until we find Hal,” Ranger said. “And it’s not that bad. Stretch makes an effort to keep things clean, but it’s an old building in a rat-infested neighborhood.”

I switched all the lights on, and Raymond walked in.

"I would not be here on a Sunday if I could find someone to sell me a green card," Raymond said. "I would find work at a superior establishment."

"I thought you had a green card, but you lost it," I said.

"Yes. That is what I meant. I lost my green card and I cannot find someone to sell me another. Soon I fear I will not even be able to buy the recreational drugs that are flowing freely from Mexico. I will pay much more for them when they must come from Colorado."

Stretch ambled through the door. "Sorry I'm late," he said. "I had a hard time convincing myself to come to work."

"That is exactly my point of view," Raymond said.

A little before five Lula and Ella arrived.

"I was torn between being an Internet sensation and taking a day off from the limelight today," Lula said. "Being a celebrity has its downsides. I can't be a bitch without it showing up on somebody's Twitter feed. What's with that? Maybe I was tired of standing in line at the checkout while some moron couldn't figure out how to find a barcode."

"So, you decided to be an Internet sensation anyway?" I said.

"Hell, no. I'm in my looking-normal clothes."

"They have a lot of sequins, and your hair is purple and green," I said.

"Yeah, but the sequins are on a tank top. That's like dressing down. It's not even like I'm wearing my going-to-church clothes."

"You go to church?"

"Hell, yes. You go to hell if you don't go to church. Everybody knows that. I've been born again a bunch of times. I don't take no chances. I believe in getting saved. I'm like a big Jesus fan."

"I'm sort of a Catholic."

"That's okay," Lula said. "It's not as good as being a Baptist, but it's better than nothing. Us Baptists got better music. We got a relationship with Jesus on account of he gets down with us."

"I have heard this," Raymond said. "I personally am Hindu on occasion, but I have heard Jesus is a cool dude."

Customers began straggling in around six o'clock. Not the numbers we'd seen for the last two days, but the tables and booths were filled. We'd recorded a message that the deli was no longer taking phone orders, so Lula was able to help wait tables.

"I got a number eighteen up," Stretch yelled.

"Not me," I said.

"Not me neither," Lula said.

Stretch leaned out, over the counter. "This looks like Lula writing."

"Yeah, but I don't need a number eighteen," Lula said. "I need a number sixteen."

"You wrote eighteen," Stretch said.

"I wrote sixteen," Lula said. "You need glasses."

"You need to learn to write," Stretch said.

Lula snatched the eighteen from the service counter and

held it out to the room. "Who wants this number eighteen, half price?"

A hand went up at one of the front tables.

"Sold to the bald idiot with big ears," Lula said.

By nine o'clock it had become obvious that Lula and I were even worse at waiting tables than we were at being bounty hunters.

"This has been a demoralizing experience," Lula said. "Tomorrow I'm going back to making sandwiches, where I know I excel. Ella can be the waitress. And while we're discussing tomorrow . . . how many tomorrows are we going to have to work here? I got an image to uphold as a bounty hunter. And I don't want my bounty hunter skills to go rusty."

I wasn't worried about my image or my skills. I knew they both sucked.

We did the evening cleanup and Ranger took the garbage to the dumpster while I watched on the monitor. He walked out, threw the bag in, and took a moment to check his iPhone. He looked around and returned to the deli.

"This isn't working," I said to Ranger.

"It's only been two days," Ranger said. "Have patience."

I locked up, and Ranger drove me to Morelli's house.

"You're the deli manager," Ranger said, idling at the curb, behind Morelli's SUV. "You need to hire a waitress."

"Are you making a comment on my waitressing skills?"

"Babe," Ranger said. "You have no waitressing skills."

Morelli was asleep on the couch when I walked in. Bob was

curled up in the recliner. He lifted his head, gave a single bark, and went back to sleep.

"Hey," I said to Morelli. "I'm home."

He sat up and blinked at me. "How'd it go? Were you kidnapped?"

"Nope. No one was kidnapped. I think between Ranger's surveillance and the police presence, this guy has been driven underground."

"He's not underground," Morelli said. "He's just moving in a different direction. He's playing with us."

Damn, I thought. I wish I'd said that.

# CHAPTER SIXTEEN

I STUMBLED INTO the Rangeman lobby at six o'clock Monday morning. I took the elevator to Ranger's apartment, let myself in, and crawled into bed. I woke up two hours later when Ranger appeared with coffee for me.

"If you're going to stay in bed, I'll get undressed and join you," Ranger said.

"I'm not undressed," I said.

"I can take care of that," Ranger said.

I got out of bed and took the coffee from him. "What's new?" I asked.

"CSI tells us the extra shoes in the apartment have never been worn."

"That's good," I said. "It means there aren't undiscovered victims out there."

I went to the kitchen, toasted a bagel, and buttered it.

"I need to go to the office this morning," I said. "I need to check in with Connie. And I need to go to my apartment to get clothes, and to make sure Rex is okay. Mrs. Delgado is looking in on him, but I want to make sure he has fresh water and enough food."

"I have a full morning here, so I'm sending you out with Luis," Ranger said. "He's new. And he's young. Try to keep him away from Lula."

"How young is he?"

"He's legal. I just want him to keep his mind on the job. Some of my men have trouble concentrating when they're around Lula."

"Shocking! And you?"

"I don't have a problem with Lula." He reached out, pulled me close against him, and kissed me. "You're my distraction."

The first kiss was playful. The next kiss lingered and deepened, and a rush of desire shot through me.

"Oh boy," I said. "This isn't good."

"You have a problem?"

"Yes!"

"Do you want me to solve it?"

"No!"

"I'm running out of time," Ranger said.

"Do you mean now or forever?"

"Now. I'm supposed to be at a meeting."

"So, you weren't intending to follow through?"

His hands slipped under my T-shirt and moved up my rib cage to my breasts. "I can cancel the meeting."

"Ummmmm," I said.

Ranger removed a hand from my breast and went for his iPhone.

"Wait," I said.

"Babe."

"I'm conflicted."

A text message dinged on his iPhone.

"Is that your meeting?" I asked.

"Yes. We'll pick this up at a better time. Finish your bagel. Luis will be waiting for you in the control room."

This is definitely for the best, I thought. Probably.

Easy to spot Luis when I entered the control room. He was the fresh-faced kid who was clearly nervous. And he had good reason to be nervous. If anything bad happened to me on his watch, his days at Rangeman would be over. I'm sure everyone else in the room was relieved that they were spared the job of guarding my body.

Luis was just under six feet with Hispanic coloring and the body of an athlete as opposed to a gym monkey. I introduced myself, and he stood at military attention.

"Pleased to meet you, ma'am," he said.

"Not 'ma'am,'" I said. "Stephanie."

"Yes, ma'am, Stephanie, ma'am," he said.

The other men were hunched over their computers, not making eye contact, trying not to laugh out loud.

We took the elevator to the underground garage, signed out a fleet SUV, and Luis drove me to my apartment. He followed me to the second floor and waited while I unlocked my door.

"Should I come in?" he asked.

"Would you like to come in?"

"Ranger said I'm not supposed to let you out of my sight."

"That's going to be awkward since I'm going to take a shower."

"Yes, ma'am, Stephanie," he said. "I'll wait right here in the hall."

I went to the kitchen and tapped on Rex's cage. He poked his head out of his soup can den, blinked his tiny black eyes at me, and retreated back into his bedding. His water bottle was full, and his food cup was half full of hamster food. I dropped a peanut and a couple Froot Loops into the cage and told him I loved him.

Twenty minutes later I was showered, dressed in clean clothes, and had a tote bag filled with enough overnight essentials for a couple days. I told Rex to be nice to Mrs. Delgado even though she had five cats, I locked my apartment, and I steered Luis to the stairs.

"Next stop is the bail bonds office on Hamilton Avenue," I told Luis.

Traffic was light, and the weather was perfect. There was still a chill in the air, but by noon it be would in the high seventies. I was feeling good in my fleece sweatshirt, sitting in the immaculate Rangeman SUV.

"This is going to be a good day," I said to Luis. "I have a feeling. Everything is going to go right today."

"Yes, ma'am, Stephanie, ma'am," he said.

Luis parked at the curb in front of the office and followed me in. Connie was at her desk, and Lula was at the coffee machine.

"Well, look at who we got here," Lula said to Luis. "Hello, cutie. What's your name?"

"Luis, ma'am."

"I'm not no 'ma'am,' but I appreciate the respect," Lula said.

"Yes, ma'am," Luis said.

Lula shook her head. "He's a hunk of love, but I'm guessing he's dumb as a box of rocks."

"This is Lula, and this is Connie," I said to Luis. "You can call them Lula and Connie."

"We got donuts on Connie's desk if you want some," Lula said. "The good ones are all gone, so we'd appreciate if you'd eat the lame ones that are left."

"Ranger doesn't like us to eat donuts," Luis said.

"Hunh," Lula said. "You do everything Ranger tells you to do?"

"Yes," Luis said.

Vinnie's office door banged open, and Vinnie looked out at us.

"It's about time you showed up," Vinnie said to me. "Where's

Waggle? Just because I got kidnapped don't mean you can stop working."

"Excuse me?" I said, eyes narrowed.

"Yeah, excuse us," Lula said. "We've been working at your dumb-ass deli. And on top of that we went after Waggle, and I got shot in the hair. You got some nerve accusing us of not working."

"Just get Waggle," Vinnie said. "I got Harry up my ass."

"Least it's something you enjoy," Lula said.

Vinnie growled and slammed and locked his door.

"We have a couple hours," I said to Lula. "I guess we could try to find Waggle."

"I'm game," Lula said, hanging her bag on her shoulder. "But I couldn't help notice you said we could *try* to find Waggle. That don't show a lot of confidence. That's a different attitude to 'Let's go get the sonnovabitch.' I got a more aggressive frame of mind, being that I need to avenge my hairdo getting ruined."

"You're right," I said. "Let's go get the sonnovabitch. First stop is the deli so I can open the door. Second stop is Food Stuff. Hopefully Russel Frick is working."

Luis drove us to the deli, and I hopped out and gave the key to Stretch.

"You are now the official keeper of the key," I said.

"I don't want the key," he said. "The key would imply manager, and managers have a short shelf life here."

"I think that's over. I haven't been snatched and Ranger

wasn't snatched. Besides, you don't have to take the garbage out. You're just in charge of locking and unlocking the door."

"Do I get more money?"

"No."

"Then what's the point?"

"Fine! Great! I'll give you five dollars extra every day you take charge of the key."

"Done," Stretch said.

I gave him the key, returned to the SUV, and Luis drove Lula and me to Food Stuff. We marched into the store and immediately spotted Frick.

"There he is," Lula said. "He's bagging, just like always. I'll get a cart, and we can pick up a few things and get in line."

"That's not necessary," I said. "We don't need to shop. We just want to talk to him."

"I still think we should buy something," Lula said. "A rotisserie chicken or something."

Luis was looking around as if at any moment disaster would strike.

"It's Food Stuff," I said to Luis. "You can relax."

"Yes, ma'am," he said, standing at attention, hand on his sidearm.

I went to the checkout to talk to Frick, and Lula went off to look at the chickens.

Frick stepped aside when he saw me. "I heard you had problems apprehending Victor," he said.

"It wasn't an ideal environment to make a capture."

"It's not an ideal environment for anything. You play bad music, and you could get shot. I didn't see you Friday night. I thought for sure you'd be back."

"I had other things going on," I said.

"But now you're looking for Waggle."

"Yes."

"I haven't got anything to tell you," Frick said. "He went home with a girl named Jillian. She's a regular. He's probably moved on to someone else by now. I don't usually see him between gigs. Once in a while I run into him at Skoogie's office when we need to pick up a check. We don't make anything from Snake Pit, but Skoogie schedules private events. Mostly fraternity parties."

"Do you have any private events coming up?"

"Later in the month. Football season."

"Did Victor and Skoogie have anything else going on? A personal relationship? A sideline business?"

"I don't know about that. Victor was interested in doing some acting, if you call that a sideline business. He wanted Skoogie to sell a reality show about the band, but nothing ever came of it. Victor was big on reality shows. Some of his ideas were pretty freaky."

"Victor seems a little unhinged," I said.

"He has his moments," Frick said.

Lula bustled up with her cart. "They didn't have any chickens out yet, and I didn't like what I was seeing with the cakes, but I found the new copy of *Star* magazine."

Lula paid for her magazine, we left Food Stuff, and I told Luis to drive to the Hamilton Building on State Street.

"That's where the agent's got an office," Lula said from the back seat. "Why are we going there again?"

"Because I have a good feeling about today. And because I have time to kill."

Luis parked in a lot half a block from the building. We walked the short distance, took the elevator to the second floor, and walked to the end of the hall. The door to Skoogie's office was open, and his assistant was standing at her desk, looking confused. She gave a yelp of surprise when we walked in. She recognized me and clapped a hand over her heart.

"Good heavens," she said. "You startled me."

"Is everything okay?" I asked.

"I don't know. Probably. If you're looking for Mr. Skoogie, I'm afraid he isn't here."

"Is he still on that business trip?" Lula asked.

"No. He returned this weekend. I actually expected him to be here by now. When I arrived this morning, the front door was unlocked, and Mr. Skoogie's office door was open. I thought he probably came in early and went out for coffee or a bagel, but he hasn't returned." Her eyes flicked to the open inner office door.

Lula and I went to the door and peeked in.

"Looks to me like he's using his shoe for a paperweight," Lula said. "That's not real sanitary. You don't know what that shoe's stepped in."

"He's never done that before," the assistant said. "I'm not sure what to make of it."

"Have you tried reaching him on his cellphone?" I asked.

"Yes. He's not picking up."

"Is there a Mrs. Skoogie?"

"No. He's divorced. Three times."

"Are there security cameras in this building?"

"In the lobby."

Lula looked over at me. "I know what you're thinking, and you don't even want to go there. Besides, where's the dumpster? There's always supposed to be a dumpster."

I called Morelli and told him about Skoogie and the shoe. "I'm probably jumping to conclusions," I said, "but I thought you might want to have someone check the security camera in the lobby to see if Skoogie was here this morning."

Luis raised his hand. "Excuse me, ma'am, Stephanie. Rangeman provides security for this building. We would monitor the camera in the lobby."

"Never mind," I said to Morelli. "Problem solved."

"Do you want me to send someone over to bag the shoe?"

"Not yet. I'll close the door to his office, and let you know what Ranger finds on the rewind. It's not as if this perfectly fits the pattern."

I called Ranger and asked him to check the video.

"This guy really likes himself," Lula said, looking at the photos on the wall. "His private office here is filled with pictures, and he's in just about all of them. He's got pictures of himself with Mickey Mouse and Beyoncé and Bill Clinton and Keith Richards and Richard Simmons. And there's lots of pictures with people I don't know. Here's one of him standing in front of the deli."

"Mr. Skoogie used to eat at the deli all the time when it was owned by Mr. Sitz," the assistant said. "They were good friends. They were roommates in college."

It was like getting hit in the face with a pie.

*"Shazam,"* Lula said.

I called Morelli back. "Come bag the shoe," I said. "There's a connection."

I got a text message from Ranger. *Skoogie arrived at 7:10 a.m. Took elevator. Never left.*

"Is there another way off this floor?" I asked the assistant. "Are there fire stairs?"

"By the elevator," she said.

"Do they go to the lobby?"

"I don't know," she said. "I've never used them."

"What about this door in the corner?" Lula asked. "Is it a way out?"

"It's a coat closet," the assistant said.

Lula opened the door and a man fell out. He had a knife stuck in his neck, and he looked surprised.

*"Holy cow!"* Lula said, jumping back.

The assistant shrieked and fainted.

I was sucking air and trying not to look. The bagel I'd had for breakfast felt like it was halfway up my throat.

Luis was the only one who didn't look like he was going to throw up. He took a throw pillow from the two-seater couch in Skoogie's office and put it under the assistant's feet. He was young, but he wasn't a lightweight, I thought.

"He's *dead,*" Lula said. "*I hate dead.* And he brushed against me. And now I have dead cooties. I got the creepy-crawly dead cooties. I need something. I need a donut. Who's got a donut?"

"I have a granola bar in my bag," I said.

"That's not the same as a donut," Lula said. "It doesn't have the same therapeutic value."

I made another call to Morelli.

"Where are you?" I asked.

"I'm at my desk. I'm finishing something up, and then I'll grab a uniform and come collect the shoe."

"Okay, but there's a d-d-dead guy here now, so could you hurry a little?"

"A dead guy?"

"I think it might be Leonard Skoogie, and he has a knife in his neck and a number two written on his forehead in black marker."

"I'm on my way."

The assistant had her eyes open and was coherent.

"What's your name?" Luis asked her.

"Miriam," she said.

"Stay down for a couple minutes more," Luis said to Miriam. "It's all okay."

"It's not okay," she said. "Mr. Skoogie is . . . you know."

"He's dead!" Lula said. "God sakes, the man is dead. And all I got is a granola bar."

Miriam looked over at Lula. "Did you know him?"

"Nope. Never met the man, but I feel for him just the same. I hate dead with a vengeance. Far as I'm concerned nothing good ever comes from being dead. And then there's the cooties." Lula gave a shiver. *"Horrible."*

I was starting to get it together. The bagel was sitting lower in my chest, and my heart rate was normalizing. I didn't know Skoogie, but seeing him crumpled and lifeless made me feel sad, and there was revulsion over the violence of his death.

"You're a good man in a crisis situation," I said to Luis.

"I'm from Chicago," he said. "We have stabbings like this all the time in my neighborhood. Only difference is there's usually lots of blood."

I forced myself to look at Skoogie. Luis was right. There was no blood. None on the floor of the office and very little on Skoogie. He had a knife sticking out of his neck, but there wasn't the bleeding I would expect to see. I was pretty sure I knew what this meant.

"He didn't die from the knife wound," I said.

Luis nodded. "That would be my guess. He'd already been dead long enough for his heart to stop pumping blood."

"That's creepy."

"Not something you see every day," Luis said.

Miriam was on her feet. "What should we do? Should we cover him, or something?"

"It's a crime scene," I said. "We should move into the other room and leave this room untouched."

I got everyone into the outer office, and I checked my watch. The deli was open for lunch. I called Ranger and filled him in.

"Is Ella at the deli?" I asked him.

"Yes. I sent her over at eleven-thirty. I haven't heard from her, so I assume everything is okay."

"I don't feel comfortable leaving here until the police arrive," I said. "I'm probably going to miss lunch, but I'll be there for dinner."

"When you're done with the police, you should come to Rangeman and look at the video to see if you recognize anyone passing through the lobby."

# CHAPTER SEVENTEEN

MORELLI STOOD HANDS on hips, staring down at Skoogie. The medical examiner was on one knee, getting a closer look. The police photographer and two EMT guys were waiting behind Morelli. Someone said the CSI van and the local news satellite truck were on the street. Miriam was at her desk in a Valium stupor.

"It's getting crowded in here," I said to Morelli. "I'm going to round up my posse and head out."

"Are you working again tonight?"

"Yes."

"I'll wait up."

We dropped Lula off at the deli, and Luis and I went on to Rangeman. I left Luis in the control room, and I walked down the short hall to Ranger's office.

"I'll run the video on a wall monitor," Ranger said. "The Hamilton Building is a budget account. One surveillance camera in the lobby, and we do a drive-by four times a day. The surveillance camera isn't monitored live. It's set to record on a forty-eight-hour loop. The front desk is manned five days a week, from six in the morning until eight in the evening. The attendant unlocks the front door when he arrives and locks it when he leaves. The tenants have keys for all other access."

I sat in one of the chairs in front of Ranger's desk and swiveled toward the bank of flat screens.

"I have this programmed to run fast until the camera picks up motion in the lobby," Ranger said. "Let me know if you want me to slow down or if you want to see something again. I'm going to run it forward from late Saturday morning. Not a lot of activity in the building over the weekend so this won't take long."

People began arriving shortly after the attendant opened the doors on Monday. I didn't recognize anyone. They all looked legitimate, carrying to-go coffee containers and dressed for business.

Skoogie entered the lobby at ten minutes after seven. A messenger bag hung from his shoulder, and he had his hand wrapped around a Starbucks coffee container. He gave a nod to the attendant and went to the elevator.

"He's starting his day early," I said. "His assistant doesn't come in until nine o'clock."

There was a steady stream of people coming and going.

When the clock on the video read twenty minutes past eight I told Ranger to stop the action. Victor Waggle was in the lobby. He was wearing a khaki knapsack and carrying a guitar case. The snake tattoo was clearly visible on his neck. He looked like he'd slept on the street. And he looked angry, striding to the elevator, talking to himself and gesturing.

"That's Victor Waggle," I said. "He's one of Skoogie's clients. He's lead guitar and vocal for Rockin' Armpits. And he's FTA. I've been looking for him. He stabbed two people on State Street a couple weeks ago."

Ranger ran the video to the end. Waggle left the building at eight forty-seven, still looking nuts. Miriam came in at nine o'clock. I didn't recognize anyone else.

"We know Waggle is handy with a knife," I said. "The big question is . . . why would he stab a dead man in the neck and hide him in the closet?"

"I'm more interested in a possible connection to the deli kidnappings," Ranger said. "I don't know if the stabbing is even relevant. I think the relationship between Skoogie and Sitz might be worth something. And I want to know if they find Waggle's prints on the shoe that was left on the desk."

"Do you think Sitz is behind the kidnappings?"

"Something to consider," Ranger said.

"Who's babysitting me this afternoon?" I asked.

"I am," Ranger said. "Before we head out I'd like to read through your file on Victor Waggle."

I gave him my file and wandered off to the control room

kitchen. Ella keeps the kitchen stocked with sandwiches, salads, and fruit. I grabbed a ham and cheese on multigrain and a water, and returned to Ranger's office to eat my lunch.

"I can't believe Vinnie wrote a bond on this guy," Ranger said. "He has no assets, no ties to the community, no real address, no relatives between here and Wisconsin. I pulled a report on him, and he has no credit history and no work history. How does he live?"

"Groupie girls. He's a local, cult-type rock star, and he sleeps around. It's one of the reasons I can't find him. If he was homeless he'd at least have a favorite doorstep or a tent under the bridge. This guy just keeps moving around from one girl to the next."

"And Leonard Skoogie was his agent and manager?"

"Yes. My best source for information is the band's drummer, but he doesn't know much about Waggle. It's not like the band hangs out together in their free time."

Ranger closed his computer and stood. "I want to see Skoogie's office, and then I want to see the Snake Pit building. Let's go for a ride."

Ranger drove to the Hamilton Building and went directly to the underground garage entrance. He slid his keycard into the machine, and the gate rolled up.

"Luis didn't know about the garage," I said.

"He doesn't have access. We don't patrol the inside of the building or the garage."

"But you have access."

"I'm special," Ranger said.

Ranger parked, and we took the elevator to the second floor. Morelli was still in Skoogie's office when Ranger and I walked in.

"What have we got?" Ranger asked Morelli.

"Speculation until the autopsy. Blunt trauma to the back of the head. Fresh needle injection site on left arm. Time of death estimated to be seven-thirty A.M."

"Could the head injury be the result of a fall?"

"The positioning is inconsistent with a fall, but it's not completely ruled out."

"So shortly after he arrived in his office he might have been knocked out and injected with something that killed him."

"That's the current thinking, but again, it's conjecture. It could also be that he injected himself, had a catastrophic reaction, and fell."

"What about the knife sticking out of his neck?" Ranger asked.

"He was actually stabbed several times. All postmortem."

"Ranger ran the security video for me, and I recognized Victor Waggle," I said to Morelli. "Waggle entered the building at eight-twenty this morning and left a half hour later. He looked angry. He kind of stormed in, waving his hands around and talking to himself."

"I'll send someone out to pick him up for questioning," Morelli said.

Ranger and I exchanged glances.

"What?" Morelli said.

"He could be hard to find," I said. "He hasn't got an address."

"This is the guy who stabbed those two people on State Street, right? He has a snake tattoo on his neck. It's not like he's unrecognizable."

"True," I said.

Ranger smiled.

"Do you mind if I look around?" he asked Morelli.

"Try not to trip over CSI."

Ranger studied the photographs on the wall. He looked out the window. He looked at the desktop. Multi-line phone, desk clock engraved to the happy couple from Aunt Tootsie, and a couple pens. Ranger pulled on gloves and went through drawers and file cabinets. He examined the locks on the doors. He went back to Morelli.

"We're heading out," Ranger said. "I'll send you a copy of the video."

"Appreciate it," Morelli said. "And remember she has a ten o'clock curfew."

Another smile from Ranger.

We walked the hall and took the stairs to the garage.

"Is there a way to get into the garage without a keycard?" I asked.

"No."

"So, we can assume the killer had a front door key or a keycard."

"Yes, but there are a lot of them floating around. This isn't a secure building. Some of the tenants prefer it that way. They can bring clients up through the garage after hours and no one knows."

Ranger left the garage and drove the length of Stark Street. He idled in front of the Snake Pit building.

"You've been here," he said.

"I was here with Lula and Hal."

"Waggle gives this as his address. Is that possible?"

"It's just a shell. And this is a scary part of Stark."

Ranger pulled to the curb and parked. "Let's take a look."

I got out and stood away from the SUV. It was Ranger's personal Porsche Cayenne. It looked and smelled new. It was black. It was immaculate. And with a tap on his remote it was electrified.

"On Thursdays and Fridays when they have music here, the street is closed off and there are food trucks and big searchlights. I don't know how they power the lights," I said.

"Let's go inside."

The inside had been swept clean. No left-behind drug paraphernalia, no empty beer bottles, no wasted snowflakes.

"That's the stage at the far end?" Ranger asked.

"Yes. The bands enter and exit through the door on the left."

We walked toward the stage, and there was a bloodcurdling shriek from the street.

"Jeez Louise," I said. "What was that?"

"I imagine someone tried to steal the Porsche."

"Will they be okay?"

"Probably. I didn't have it set on lethal."

Ranger went out the side door and looked at the area behind the building. He walked down the alley to the street.

The Porsche was still parked at the curb. No other car in sight. No Porsche stealers lurking. Ranger clicked the security system off, but I kept my distance.

"You first," I said.

Ranger opened the door and got behind the wheel. I touched a finger to the SUV. I didn't get shocked, so I got in next to him.

"Babe," he said, "you have trust issues."

"Better safe than sorry."

"Sometimes safe isn't fun."

"I didn't know you were that interested in fun."

"Spend the night with me and judge for yourself," Ranger said.

Here's the thing. I've spent the night with him and *fun* isn't the first word that comes to mind. The first word would be *WOW* or maybe *YUM* or *AHHHHHHH, YES!* Okay, that's two words, but he's worth two words and more. Truth is, he's magic. And he's also major trouble in the romance department since Morelli isn't keen on sharing me. For that matter, I'm not keen on sharing either. Being in love and in a relationship with one man is complicated enough. Being in love and in a relationship with two men would be suicide. But it's hard not to be in love after a night of magic.

"You promised Morelli you'd have me home by my curfew."

"Wrong. Morelli told me to get you home by ten o'clock. *I* didn't promise anything."

The magic thing got me to thinking about Wulf. "What do you suppose Wulf's role is in all this?" I asked.

"I think it's tangential. Wulf is looking for someone who happens to be involved."

"Nothing more?"

"Probably nothing more in the beginning, but that could have changed. If Wulf is intrigued by the game he might join in."

It was a beautiful day. Full-on sunshine and seventy degrees. I was in the SUV next to Ranger, and I was thinking about the beach. Forty-five minutes away. I wanted to push all thoughts about the deli aside, spread a blanket on the sand, and lay there listening to the surf, feeling the sun on my face.

"We should go to Point Pleasant," I said. "We could lay on the beach and hold hands."

"Babe," Ranger said.

His voice was soft and wistful. Okay, *wistful* might be a stretch for Ranger, but there was a quality there that wasn't familiar. Or maybe I was just projecting my own feelings. God knows, I felt wistful.

We were halfway down Stark, almost to State Street, and Ranger pulled to the curb.

"We can't go to the beach," he said. "Is there something else? Would you like an ice cream cone? Flowers? A kitten?"

"A kiss," I said.

He leaned across the console and kissed me. Gentle. Loving. Wistful.

"Thanks," I said. "I feel better now."

"Anytime," he said.

Lula was on a rant when we got to the deli.

"I can't work under these conditions," Lula said, arms waving in the air. "There's no condiments. How am I supposed to create my art burgers and nuevoninis without no condiments?"

"What's a 'nuevonini'?" I asked.

"It's when I use the panini machine to fabulitize an ordinary plain-ass sandwich," Lula said. "My peeps have expectations."

"Why don't we have any condiments?"

"On account of nobody ordered any," Lula said.

"You're using hot sauce and mayo like it was water," Stretch said. "How am I supposed to know we're out of everything? It's not like I'm the manager here."

Everyone looked over at me.

"What?" I said.

"You are the manager," Raymond said. "You are the place where the buck stops. You should be more diligent in your job. If you were doing your job we would not have to listen to this large woman going bat-shitty."

"You're right," I said. "I promise I'll take inventory tonight. Give me a list and I'll make a store run."

Lula glared at Raymond, her hands on her hips. "What do you mean by 'large woman'? Are you making some politically incorrect comment on my size? Are you engaging in body shaming?"

"You are a big woman," Raymond said. "It is a fact."

"I'm not tall, though," Lula said.

"No, you are not tall," Raymond said. "You are robust."

"Okay," Lula said. "I can live with that."

Customers were beginning to trickle in. Ella was serving water and distributing menus. Lula gave me her list.

"Anyone else want to add to the list?" I asked.

"I would like a nubile virgin," Raymond said. "You can surprise me on the sexual orientation."

Ranger was smiling again.

"I've never seen you smile this much," I said.

"Babe, your life is a train wreck."

# CHAPTER EIGHTEEN

MY SHOPPING CART was filled with ketchup, mustard, mayo, hot sauce, horseradish, barbecue sauce, bags of chips, white bread, and cans of cranberry sauce. I pushed it to the checkout, and while I was standing in line I noticed a guy walking through the store, carrying a handbasket. He was wearing a hoodie and a ball cap, and he had a snake tattoo on his neck.

I grabbed Ranger's sleeve. "I think that's Waggle! I saw his tattoo."

We stepped out of line and walked toward the guy with the tattoo. He was heading down the aisle with the cooking oil, vinegar, pasta, and marinara sauce. He was sauntering along, checking out the oils, pausing to read ingredients. Ranger and I moved behind him.

"Victor Waggle?" I asked.

The guy turned and looked around, wide-eyed. "Where? Where is he?"

"Sorry," I said. "I saw the snake tattoo, and I thought you were Waggle."

"I wish," he said. "The dude's awesome. My snake is different from his. I got a cobra. He has a rattler."

"Did you get this at Eddie's on Stark Street?" Ranger asked.

"Yeah. Eddie does the best snakes. Victor got his snake there too."

"Do you know Victor?" I asked.

"No. Do you?"

"Not as well as I'd like to know him," I said.

The guy grinned. "That's what all the girls say. They all want his seed."

"I don't suppose you know where I could find him," I said.

"Naw. Sorry. I hear he floats around."

"Spreading his seed," I said.

"Exactly!"

Ranger and I went back to the checkout.

"I have to give you points," I said to Ranger. "You kept a straight face through the whole seed-spreading conversation."

"It wasn't easy," Ranger said. "Points to you too. I thought you did an excellent job of indicating you might want seed."

"I'm a professional," I said. "All part of being a bounty hunter."

We brought our bags of ketchup and mayo and whatever back to the deli and dumped them in the pantry.

"Where's the chips?" Lula said. "I need chips. I'm having a

meltdown here. I can't make my world-famous Spam Chip Burger without no chips."

"Someone wants a Spam Chip Burger?" I asked. "It's not even on the menu. I didn't know we even had Spam."

"They wanted a tuna sandwich on rye but that's lame. I can't give those poor people tuna on rye. I got more pride than that."

I stocked Lula up on chips and an assortment of condiments and went back to Ranger.

"Things seem to be going okay," I said. "We've gone back to the normal number of customers."

"I want to talk to Eddie. Tell your crew we'll be back by closing."

Eddie's Tattoos was on the second block of Stark. It was a great location because it was next to a popular bar. People got drunk and they got a tattoo.

The second block of Stark was respectable enough to require only the standard SUV security of a deafening alarm. We parked and walked half a block back to Eddie's. It was still early in the day for tattoos, and Eddie was alone in his shop.

Eddie was a rangy guy in his fifties who was covered in tattoos. His hair was gray and pulled into a ponytail. He obviously knew Ranger because they did one of those elaborate man-greetings with the knuckle bumps and hand-clasping routines.

"I see you got your old lady with you," Eddie said. "You want her inked?"

"Not today," Ranger said. "I'm looking for Victor Waggle."

"Good luck, bro. Nobody ever knows where to find that dude. He floats."

"Does he have friends?" Ranger asked.

"Everyone's his friend, and no one's his friend."

"I need a place to start."

"The Snake Pit."

"Been there," Ranger said.

"His manager is around the corner on State."

"Manager's dead," Ranger said.

"I hadn't heard. Was it recent?"

Ranger nodded.

"Victor's gotta be broken up about that," Eddie said. "They had some kind of a project going. A movie or a TV show."

"Does Victor have a lot of tattoos?" I asked. "It sounds like you talk to him frequently."

"It's the snake," Eddie said. "His fans all want the snake around their neck. Victor gets a commission for everyone he brings in here. I do one or two a week."

"Let me know if you see him," Ranger said.

They did another ritual goodbye thing, and we left the shop.

"You didn't even pay him off," I said.

"I helped him get rid of some parasites last year."

"Ringworm?"

"Fire and personal injury insurers."

"Will they continue to leave him alone?"

"They're out of business. They've relocated."

I wasn't always sure what that meant with Ranger. It could

mean they moved to North Carolina, or it could mean they were encased in cement at the bottom of the Delaware River.

"Where do we go from here?" I asked.

"Rangeman. I want to do some research on Leonard Skoogie. It won't take long."

Ranger grabbed a kale smoothie from the control room kitchen and took it to his office. If I'd been at the deli I would have tried the Spam Chip Burger. Since I was at Rangeman, I settled for grilled chicken in a spinach wrap. I ate at one of the small bistro tables in the kitchen area and watched the handful of men who were answering phones and watching monitors. Conversation among them was minimal and too soft for me to clearly hear. Once in a while something would beep or a blue diode would flash on a desktop. I finished my wrap and went in search of a cookie. No cookies in sight. The triathletes who worked at Rangeman ate fruit for dessert. I wasn't up for fruit so I went back to Ranger's office.

"How's it going?" I asked.

"Leonard Skoogie and Ernie Sitz were college roommates. Six months after graduation, Skoogie moved to L.A. and bounced around as an extra, a production assistant, tried script writing. Got a job as a producer for a game show that was cancelled three days after he started. Represented one of the women who was a prize presenter on the show. Got her a few small acting roles. Acquired a second actress. Two years into his career as a talent agent he was arrested for procuring prostitution. He got off with a wrist slap and moved to New York. Eventually he found his way to Trenton and resumed his friendship with Ernie Sitz. It looks like he made a decent income from repping bands for frat parties and magicians for kids' birthday parties, but so far as I can tell he's never had a real success. And his three failed marriages were costly to dissolve. He partnered up with Sitz to produce a play, but it closed off Broadway."

I'm a bounty hunter, barely scraping by, so I'm no one to judge, but it sounded to me like Leonard Skoogie was chasing a dream he had no chance of catching.

"Did you pull information on Sitz?"

"In an odd way, Sitz is a mirror image of Skoogie. He's made a career of reinventing himself. He's got a history of making bad choices in wives, business partners, and semi-legal investments. He ran from a racketeering charge that would have been difficult to prove and abandoned the one good piece of real estate he ever owned."

"The deli?"

"Yes."

"Speaking of the deli . . . we should get back there before the wrong person tries to take the garbage to the dumpster."

Ranger closed his computer, stood, and stretched. His T-shirt rode up exposing three inches of abs, and I almost had an orgasm.

We took the elevator to the garage, and Ranger chose his Porsche 911 Turbo. There were no parking places in front of the deli, so he drove to the alley and parked in the small back lot.

"Tempting fate?" I asked him.

"I don't think there's much risk to us or the car."

Lula and Stretch were yelling at each other when we walked in. Stretch had a spatula in his hand, and Lula was armed with a squeeze bottle of ketchup.

"He assaulted me," Lula said.

"I didn't assault you," Stretch said.

"You whacked me with the spatula!"

"That was to get your attention. You always got those earbuds in your ear. You don't hear anything anybody says to you. And if that isn't bad enough you were singing. *Loud.*"

"That is true," Raymond said. "And you are not such a good singer. It is like someone stepping on cats."

"That's 'cause I was singing to Janis Joplin, and she does a lot of screaming," Lula said. "I wouldn't have to sing if things weren't so boring around here. No one's ordering sandwiches. I haven't got anything to do."

"That is because you are a very bad sandwich maker," Raymond said. "Word has gotten out. Not even my excellent fries can save your sandwiches."

"Your French fries suck," Lula said. "You use cheapskate oil. Your fries are what's ruining my sandwich reputation."

"That is so not true," Raymond said. "I am insulted to my core."

"Get real," Stretch said. "You use the same oil all week. Remember that time when you came in and had to fish the rat out of the fry oil?"

"Oh yes," Raymond said. "That was horrifying. I had to use the big tongs."

"Excuse me," Ella said. "The gentleman at table number three is waiting for his number seventeen."

"Where's his number seventeen?" Stretch said to Lula.

"I was thinking about making it when you hit me," Lula said.

"What's to think about? It's all on the menu," Stretch said. "Why don't you stop farting around with the food and read the directions for a change? You might even make something edible."

"I don't like your attitude," Lula said.

And she squirted him in the chest with the ketchup. *SPLAT.* A big red splotch on his white chef's coat.

Stretch narrowed his eyes and smacked her on the top of her head with his spatula. Lula squirted more ketchup and Stretch swatted the ketchup out of Lula's hand. The ketchup bottle flew through the air and landed with a splash in the fryer. There was a lot of crackling, with oil splattering onto the counter and the eight-burner gas cooktop. Flames raced in runners across the counter and up the greasy wall.

"*Fire!*" Lula yelled. "Somebody do something!"

Ranger looked around. "Where's the fire extinguisher?"

"It got very old so we threw it away," Raymond said. "We needed the space for the paper towels."

I punched 911 on my cellphone and gave them our location. Ella cleared out the remaining customers. Stretch and Ranger attempted to smother the fire with kitchen towels.

"I got it under control," Lula said. "Stand back."

She aimed the sink's handheld sprayer at the fryer, turned the water on, and *WHOOSH* the entire area exploded in flames.

"It is not a good idea to put water on a grease fire," Raymond said. "This is bad. This is very, very bad."

Ranger grabbed my wrist and yanked me to the front door. Lula, Ella, Stretch, and Raymond followed.

"I need to move my car, so the fire trucks can get in the back lot," Ranger said to me. "Stay here with everyone and don't move."

He ran down the alley between the buildings and disappeared from view. It was a two-story building, and I couldn't see in the second floor windows.

"What's up there?" I asked Stretch.

"Nothing," he said. "It was an apartment, but it hasn't been occupied in years. Sitz used it like an attic. It's full of junk."

I heard sirens and saw flashing lights a couple blocks away. It was a dark, moonless night, but the sidewalks were lit by the faux gaslight streetlamps. Late commuters and residents were standing at a distance, watching the drama unfold. Our little deli family was huddled together. Moments before we'd been squabbling, and now we were speechless. I have no idea what was going through anyone else's head, but I was numb. It happened so fast. It was hard to believe. There was smoke pouring out the door, and flames licking at windows. And out of the dumb numbness I had a moment of panic for the poor trapped roaches and rats.

Ranger moved next to me, put an arm around me, and cuddled me into him.

"Are you okay?" he asked.

"The poor roaches and rats," I said.

He kissed me on the forehead. "They're fine. They were all running out the back door when I moved my car."

"Thank God." I looked at him. "Were they really?"

"Babe," he said. "You couldn't kill those roaches with a blowtorch."

We all moved farther down the street when the trucks rolled in. The buildings on the block were brick, there were narrow alleys between them, and there was no wind, so the fire was staying contained.

"What are we to do tomorrow?" Raymond asked. "Where will I go if I have no fry station?"

"It might not be so bad," Lula said. "Things like this always look worse in the dark, what with all the flames and smoke. This is just like that grease fire Wayne Kulicki started at Eat and Go. And that stupid Eat and Go was back in business two days later."

"They're pouring a lot of water in there," Stretch said.

"Yes," Raymond said. "The number seventeen is going to be ruined."

I called Morelli and told him I would probably miss my curfew.

"We sort of burned the deli down," I said. "We're waiting to talk to one of the officials, and then Ranger will take me to your house."

"Let me talk to Ranger."

I handed my phone over to Ranger and waited while Ranger assured him I was undamaged.

There was a loud explosion from somewhere deep in the deli. The firemen took a couple steps back but continued to spray the water.

It was almost midnight when Ranger walked me to Morelli's front door and handed me over. Bob ran in from the kitchen and jumped on me, almost knocking me over. He snuffled my jeans and my shirt and licked my face.

"He thinks you're dinner," Morelli said. "You smell like fried Spam."

"It was horrible. We burned the deli down."

"On purpose?"

"No! Lula and Stretch were yelling at each other. She was squirting him with ketchup, and he was whacking her with his spatula. He whacked the ketchup bottle out of her hand, and it flew into the hot fryer. It went downhill fast after that."

"No one was hurt?"

"No people were hurt, but I imagine some rats got toasted." I looked down at myself. My sneakers were soaked and my clothes were sooty. "I need a shower."

"I'll help."

"Thanks, but I'm exhausted."

"That's okay. I'll do all the work," Morelli said. "I'm good with soap."

# CHAPTER NINETEEN

MORELLI DRAGGED ME out of bed and handed me some clothes.

"It's dark out," I said. "It's the middle of the night."

"Technically it's more the middle of the morning. Get dressed. I have coffee downstairs."

"I don't want coffee. I want to go back to bed."

"I have an early meeting, and I need to drop you off at Rangeman."

"I don't need Rangeman. There's no deli. It's over."

"It isn't over. Five men are missing, and a man is dead. The dead man wasn't on-site at the deli."

"Leonard Skoogie and Ernie Sitz were college roommates."

"Yes. And they were business partners."

"Did you get prints off Skoogie's shoe?"

"Waggle's prints were on the shoe. I'm not supposed to be telling you any of this."

"No problem. I'm too tired to remember."

Twenty minutes later I stumbled into Rangeman and took the elevator to Ranger's apartment. I shuffled to his bedroom, kicked my shoes off, and stretched out on his bed. I was instantly asleep, and when I finally opened my eyes Ranger was standing at bedside. I felt like Goldilocks in baby bear's bed.

"I'm not a morning person," I said.

Ranger was grinning. "You smell like fried Spam."

"It's in my hair. I can't get it out." I looked over at the window. The curtains were still drawn. "What time is it?"

"It's almost ten o'clock. I want to make a run to the deli and check on the damage."

I swung my legs over the side of the bed, stood, and straightened my shirt. "Morelli said Waggle's prints were on the Skoogie shoe. Does that mean anything to you?"

"It's another piece of information that will eventually make sense."

I followed him out of his apartment and down to the garage. We drove to the deli and parked. A single fire truck was still in the street plus a couple cop cars. I didn't see Morelli. There was a lot of debris on the sidewalk. Greasy runoff filled the gutters, and the air was heavy with the smell of smoke and soggy upholstery. The soot-stained building was cordoned off with crime scene tape.

"Are your men still in place?" I asked Ranger.

"No. I pulled them last night."

I saw two forlorn figures standing in the shadow of the

fire truck. Raymond and Stretch. I waved and walked over to them.

"This is a shambles," Raymond said. "And it is a tragedy that my green card was destroyed in the fire."

"That's your story?"

"I will swear to it," Raymond said.

"I guess you'll be looking for other jobs."

"No problem there," Stretch said. "There are always jobs for line cooks."

"You will have to travel to see your honey," Raymond said to Stretch.

"There are always other honeys," Stretch said.

"That is a good, positive attitude," Raymond said. "It is the presence of a good purveyor that most worries me. I will first try to find employment in an establishment serviced by Frankie."

"Freakin' A," Stretch said.

Vinnie's Cadillac jerked to a stop behind the fire truck, and Vinnie lunged out of the car.

"Shit!" Vinnie said, staring at the blackened hull that used to be the deli. "Shit, shit, shit, shit, shit!"

"Who is this vulgar man?" Raymond asked. "That is a lot of shit even for Jersey."

"He works for the guy who owns the deli," I said. "He's my boss."

Vinnie spotted me and rushed over, arms waving, eyes bulging.

"You were supposed to manage," he yelled at me. "This isn't

managing! Does this look like managing? No! This looks like Harry's investment turned into a smoking turd. Harry's gonna crap himself. And then he's gonna kill me. And it's all your fault. I put you in charge, and you burned the deli down to the ground! You're a walking clusterfuck."

Ranger moved into Vinnie's range of vision and Vinnie stopped in mid-rant. Everyone knew I was under Ranger's protection, and the possibility of angering Ranger was even more frightening than angering Harry.

"Maybe I got carried away," Vinnie said. "I mean, we're family, right? Anyway, you probably did me a favor. We had this pain-in-the-ass rat's nest overinsured."

"It was an accident," I said. "It started with a grease fire."

"Yeah, these things happen," Vinnie said. "I'll go explain it to Harry."

We all watched him scramble back into his Cadillac and drive away.

"I think I would not like to work for him," Raymond said. "He reminds me of my mother."

The alleys on both sides of the deli building were clogged with chunks of roofing material and window glass, so Ranger and I walked around the block to see the rest of the damage.

The back door was covered with plywood and crisscrossed with crime scene tape. Puddles of sooty water and pieces of charred wood littered the parking area. We were standing there, taking it in, when the Central GP truck rumbled down the alley and stopped just short of us.

Frankie got out and looked at the blackened brick. "When did this happen?" he asked.

"Last night," I said. "Grease fire."

"How bad is it?"

"We haven't been inside, but I don't think there's much left."

"So, I'm guessing you don't want your order?"

"Stretch and Raymond are in front. They might need oregano."

"I'll drive around," Frankie said.

We watched the truck move on down the alley.

"He has a nice business going," Ranger said.

I gestured at the deli. "Not much to see from the outside. And I suppose it's not safe to go in."

"We'll get notified when it's safe to go in."

"I got a text from Connie. She has two new files for me. Do you have time to take me to the office?"

"I have a meeting at three o'clock. Until then I'm all yours."

Connie was alone at her desk when Ranger and I walked in.

"Where is everyone?" I asked.

"Vinnie is talking to Harry. Lula is out foraging lunch."

"It's early for lunch," I said.

"Not for Lula," Connie said. "I'm glad you're here. I have two new court skips. One of them is a high bond, high flight risk."

I took the two files and flipped the first one open. Ranger was pressed against my back, reading over my shoulder. He was warm, and he smelled nice, and I was having a hard time concentrating on the file.

"I'll take these out to the car, and we'll get right to it," I said to Connie.

"When you're done, look for the FTA," Connie said.

The first guy was a repeater. Darren Boot. Forty-two years old. Lived with his mother in a ramshackle house by the junkyard. A couple times a year they would get crazy drunk, and Darren would go off and do something stupid. This time he'd stolen a cop car and driven it through the front window of a 7-Eleven.

The second guy was a drug dealer with gang ties. He had family and "business associates" in Guatemala and an arrest record. He'd run a light and had been pulled over by police. They found a bale of cannabis in the trunk of his car, and a suitcase filled with cocaine. In the struggle to cuff the gang guy, one of the cops suffered a groin injury and the gang guy got a broken nose and lost a couple teeth.

Ranger took the file from me and read aloud.

"Walter Jesus Santiago, AKA Wally San, AKA W. J. San, AKA Jesus Santiago, AKA Tarzan. And I saved the best for last. AKA Forest Kottel."

"I guess we should try to find Mr. Santiago," I said to Ranger.

"He gives an address of Bartlett Street. That's one block over from Stark. He's a self-employed entrepreneur, so either he's at home or else he's at the port in Perth Amboy picking up a bale."

Ranger cut across town and cruised down Bartlett. The first

five blocks were similar to Stark, but were more residential and pervasively Hispanic. Buildings were red brick, three- and four-story, some in better shape than others. The graffiti was more colorful than the Stark Street graffiti. I attributed this to more recent writing. Signs for the grocery stores and bars were in Spanish. A couple buildings on the fifth block were pockmarked with gunshots, but the first four blocks seemed relatively safe.

Santiago lived on the third block. We parked, entered the building, and took the stairs to the second floor. Two apartments. Santiago lived in the rear-facing one. Ranger knocked on the door, and it opened with the security chain in place. A young man looked out at us, and I was pretty sure it was Santiago. I could only see two inches of him, but he resembled the mug shot in his bond folder.

"Walter Santiago?" Ranger asked.

"Nah," he said. "He don't live here."

"Can I come in?" Ranger asked.

"Sure," the guy said.

The door closed, and we could hear the bolt slam into place. Ranger took a step back and said, "Bond enforcement." He gave the door a hard kick and *BANG!* The bolt snapped loose, and the door crashed open.

It appeared to be a two-room apartment. The main room had a small kitchen area to one side, a huge flat-screen TV on the opposite wall, a massive black leather couch, and two matching recliners facing the TV. The window looking out at the back alley was open, and I could see Santiago on the fire escape. A moment later he was gone.

"Clear the apartment," Ranger said, crossing the room. "I'll go after Tarzan."

I ran to the window and watched Ranger vault over the fire escape railing. He grabbed the bottom of the railing with one hand, hung for a beat, and dropped to the ground. Tarzan had climbed down the ladder and was only a few steps in front of Ranger. Ranger closed the gap, grabbed Tarzan by the back of his shirt, and threw him to the ground. In seconds, Tarzan was cuffed and back on his feet.

I went back to the bedroom and made sure no one was in the closet, under the bed, or in the bathroom. I closed the window, and closed the door as I left the apartment. Ranger was on the sidewalk, waiting for me, when I came out.

"Nice work," I said. "You should be the one named Tarzan."

"It's been a while since I chased someone down. I spend most of my time behind a desk now."

It was obvious that he also spent time in the gym because his body was perfect, and he hadn't broken a sweat capturing Tarzan. My body had to make do with good genes, because I hated the gym. My favored exercise was walking the length of the mall to get to Cinnabon. So far, I was holding my own, but I suspect the future might be ugly.

Ranger loaded Tarzan AKA Santiago AKA Forest Kottel into the back seat of his SUV, and we drove him to the police station. We dumped him off, I got my body receipt, and we went back to the office to turn the receipt in to Connie.

"Thanks," I said to Ranger. "I couldn't have captured him on my own. I'm no good at breaking down doors. I can't jump over fire escape railings. And I probably couldn't have caught up to him on the ground."

"You would have done the capture your way," Ranger said. "You would have told him you were selling Girl Scout cookies, and while he was thinking about Thin Mints and Samoas, Lula would have knocked him over and sat on him."

"Sometimes it works," I said.

"I have to get back to the office," Ranger said. "You can come back with me, or I can send one of my men to follow you around."

"Send one of your men. I want to go after Darren Boot."

Lula was sitting on the couch when I walked into the bonds office. I gave the body receipt to Connie, and I took a piece of the pizza that was on her desk.

"I have to find Darren Boot," I said.

"I'll come with you," Lula said. "Where's this Darren Boot live?"

"By the junkyard. We've been there a couple times. He lives with his mother."

"Now I remember. They're the ones with the mushroom farm. And the mother dresses up like Minnie Mouse."

# CHAPTER TWENTY

LULA DROVE THE length of Stark Street, passed the junkyard, and after a half mile we saw the rusted mailbox with BOOT painted on it. The rutted dirt driveway led to a bedraggled bungalow that was surrounded by thigh-high grass.

Lula parked, and we got out of the Firebird and set out on the narrow path to the front door. A big white chicken ran across the path in front of Lula.

"Holy heck," Lula said. "What the hell?"

All around us we could hear grass rustling and chickens clucking.

"This is freaking me out," Lula said. "I only like supermarket chickens. The naked ones with no feathers. And I prefer them shrink-wrapped and air-chilled and previously fed non-GMO shit."

I preferred them as frozen and breaded nuggets or else cooked by my mother.

"Watch where you're walking," I said. "You don't want to step on a chicken or whatever it leaves behind."

"That's a disgusting thought," Lula said. "I got on my open-toe fashionista gladiator shoes."

We reached the rickety front stoop, and I knocked on the door. Minnie Mouse answered on the second knock.

"Mrs. Boot," I said. "Perhaps you remember me. I'm Stephanie Plum."

Darlene Boot was sixty-seven years old, five feet two inches tall, and had a shape like an apple. Skinny legs encased in black tights. Short curly gray hair held in place by a red and white polka-dotted Minnie Mouse bow with mouse ears. The dress was straight from vintage Disney. Black top and fluffy red skirt with more white polka dots. Short puffy sleeves. Finished off with bright yellow rubber boots that I'm sure were excellent for walking behind chickens.

"Oh dear," she said. "I suppose you're here to repossess Darren."

"Is he home?"

"No. I'm so sorry. He had some errands to run."

"What sort of errands?" I asked.

"He was going to the feed store. It's somewhere across the river. And then he was going to gas up the truck and get some beer. The chickens like a little beer now and again."

"I see you still got the Minnie Mouse thing going," Lula said.

Darlene smiled. “Sometimes I wear one of the princess dresses, but I like Minnie the best.”

“Yeah,” Lula said. “You can’t go wrong with Minnie. Do you know you got a lot of chickens running around out there in your front yard? What’s with that?”

“It’s our new business,” Darlene said. “The mushrooms didn’t work out, so we’re trying chickens. Would you like to come in and have a cup of tea while you wait for Darren?”

We stepped inside and froze. Wire cages filled with roosting chickens were stacked everywhere, and a bunch of chickens were meandering around, pecking at the furniture.

“These are our egg producers,” Darlene said. “We’re real proud of them.”

“What about the outside chickens?” Lula asked, keeping her eyes on the meandering chickens.

“We sort of lost control over them,” Darlene said. “We thought it would be nice to let them go free-range, but then we couldn’t find the eggs in the grass, and they kept multiplying. I guess you might say they’re feral chickens now.”

There was a bloodcurdling squawk from the front yard.

“What the heck was that?” Lula asked.

“We also got some feral cats,” Darlene said. “Big ones.” Especially Miss Kitty, Suzy, and Apple Puff.

“Maybe we’ll come back some other time,” I said to Darlene, giving her my card. “Tell Darren we were here, and we’ll be happy to give him a ride to the courthouse, so he can get his court date rescheduled.”

"That's real nice of you," Darlene said. "I'll pass it along."

Lula and I stood on the stoop and looked at the path to her car. There was some blood and feathers on the path, but no chicken.

"Do you think it's safe to walk there?" Lula asked me. "What if that feral cat is still hungry, and he's lurking in the grass? Or what if the chickens are planning a counterattack?"

"Like a chicken army?"

"Exactly! Chickens aren't smart. They got a brain the size of a pea. They could attack us by mistake."

"I'll chance it," I said. "I'm pretty sure I could take on a chicken."

"I saw you get attacked by a goose once, and you were screaming like a little girl."

"That was a goose. Entirely different."

We started down the path, and a big red rooster rushed out of the grass at Lula and pecked her big toe. Lula shrieked, put her foot to the rooster, and punted it about twenty feet in the air.

"I've been pecked!" she yelled. "I've been pecked." She drew her gun, and fired off a shot.

"What are you shooting at?" I asked her.

"I don't know," she said. "Reflex action."

I looked down at her foot. "I don't see any blood."

"He caught me by surprise. Lucky thing for him that he flew away and didn't get shot."

"He didn't fly away. You kicked him about a quarter of a mile. He might have done some fluttering on the descent."

A Rangeman SUV was idling behind Lula's Firebird. I didn't recognize the man at the wheel, but I waved and he waved back.

"It's strange not to be heading for the deli now," Lula said. "I don't know what I'm supposed to do with myself."

"I'm going back to the office. I want to do some research on Leonard Skoogie and Victor Waggle."

"Sounds good to me," Lula said. "I'm gonna do some research on my ancestry. I might sign up for one of those DNA kits they advertise on television. It would be fun to know more about my roots. Do you know all about your ancestors?"

"My father's side is Italian as far back as we can trace. His relatives were all farmers. Not especially successful. Always too many kids and not enough land. My great-grandparents Plumeri immigrated when they were in their twenties. They came over as indentured servants. The name was shorted on Ellis Island. My other great-grandparents met after they were already in America. My great-grandmother came with her parents. My great-grandfather stowed away on a boat and was arrested when it docked in Perth Amboy. I'm told there was some bribery involved, and he managed to walk away."

"What about on your mother's side?"

"Hungarian, mostly. There might have been some border crossings. My great-grandfather Mazur deserted from the army. We aren't sure which one. Apparently, it was a topic no one would discuss. He hopped a boat and came to America. My great-grandmother was pregnant at the time and unmarried.

The story goes that she followed my great-grandfather and put a gun to his head to marry her."

"And they lived happily ever after?"

"Grandma Mazur said my grandfather told her they fought like cats and dogs."

"See, that's what I'm talking about. You know all kinds of interesting things. All I know is that my momma was a 'ho, and I followed in her footsteps. Just about all the women in my family were professional. I don't know anything past that."

Lula parked in front of the bonds office, and the Rangeman SUV pulled in behind her. I waved at Ranger's man on my way into the office, and he gave me a thumbs-up.

"It's like you're the president or something," Lula said. "It's a wonder they don't follow you into the bathroom and check behind the shower curtain."

Connie was standing at her desk with her purse in her hand.

"You got here just in time," she said. "I was going to lock up. Vinnie is at physical therapy, and I have to go downtown to bond someone out."

*Physical therapy* was code for a nooner. Or in this case an afternooner.

"Is it okay if I use your computer?" I asked.

"Sure," Connie said. "I should be about an hour. I'll be back to close up."

Lula settled onto the couch with her iPad, and I went to

Connie's desk. I ran Skoogie through a couple programs but didn't turn up anything new.

"Here's something weird," Lula said. "I've been surfing around, checking up on my fame as a celebrity sandwich maker. There's a unflattering video of me waiting tables. And there's a couple newspaper articles and some local television pieces on how people have been disappearing and leaving their shoe behind at the deli. I asked for more on the subject, and I got a video someone made about the deli kidnapping. It's like an amateur reality-show thing. There's five of them. And one of them looks like Hal."

I looked over at her. "How much like Hal?"

"A lot like Hal."

Lula brought her iPad over and passed it to me.

I was dumbstruck. "This *is* Hal," I said.

I scrolled back, looked at all five, and also recognized Wayne Kulicki. The videos had been uploaded by someone named Hotshot. They were grainy night shots showing a man walking out of the deli's back door, carrying a garbage bag. There was a blinding flash of light and the next scene was a single shoe on the asphalt parking lot. This was followed by a visual of crime scene tape and police doing their job investigating.

I called Morelli.

"Lula stumbled across some YouTube videos that seem to be recording the deli kidnappings," I said.

"Seriously?"

"Yeah. I recognized Hal and Wayne Kulicki. You'll want to look at this."

"I'm just getting into my car to leave for the day. Are you at the office? I'll head over."

"I'll wait for you."

I called Ranger and told him about the videos.

"I got them," Ranger said, moments later. "That's Hal."

"What do you make of this? Can you trace down Hotshot?"

"Doubtful if I can trace Hotshot through YouTube, but the feds might be able, and I can hack into the feds."

"Why is this up on YouTube?" I asked.

"Someone wanted it seen."

"They wanted to get caught? They were proud of their photography? What?"

"Tell Lula to keep surfing. Maybe she'll stumble on something else."

"Morelli is on his way over to the office, and then I'll go home with him. Your guy can clock out. Tell him thank you from me."

"Babe," Ranger said. And he hung up.

It took Morelli twenty minutes to get to the office, and Connie was three minutes behind him. I had the videos on Connie's computer, and we all crowded together to look.

"I did a fast review of the kidnap victims before I left," Morelli said. "This first one is Elroy Ruiz. Age thirty-two. It's difficult to see his face in the video, but he has the right build.

The next up is Kenny Brown. The video is dark but this looks like our man. The next victim is more recognizable. He gets to the dumpster and turns toward the camera. His name is Ryan Meier. Nineteen years old. In the country on a student visa."

"Where's he from?" I asked.

"Switzerland."

I had an immediate aha! moment. Wulf is a Swiss national. This is the Wulf connection.

I advanced to the fourth video, and Wayne Kulicki walked out of the deli. He had a bag of garbage, and he didn't seem concerned. He didn't look around. Nothing caught his attention on his way to the dumpster. He tossed the bag in, turned and faced the camera, and there was the blinding flash. Next frame was of his shoe.

The last video was Hal. He walked to the dumpster, tossed the bag, turned and walked toward the camera, smiling. Flash of light. No more Hal.

"There are three different camera angles here," I said. "The first video was shot from the second floor of the deli building. That's why you can't see the manager's face. The second, third, and fourth were shot from a camera just to the right of the deli's back door at a height of about six feet. And it looks like Hal was captured on video by a camera that was placed in the dry cleaner's parking lot."

"It's like making these movies was all part of the kidnapping," Lula said. "I want to see season two where they show you what happens next."

"There's no Vinnie video," I said.

Vinnie walked in from the back entrance. "What do you mean, 'There's no Vinnie video'?"

"Lula found videos of the kidnap victims on YouTube, but you aren't included. Are you remembering anything at all from the kidnapping?" Morelli asked Vinnie.

"Bananas. Everything was black, and I kept smelling bananas."

"Was this in the beginning when you were first captured?" Morelli asked.

"I don't know. I don't remember anything except bananas." Vinnie narrowed his eyes. "I hate bananas."

Morelli made a couple calls to report the videos.

"Will you be able to trace them?" I asked him.

"Possibly. It'll get passed up the chain of command."

"What about camera placement? Do you think someone was in the building, on the second floor, for the first kidnapping?"

"Either that or they used a drone," Morelli said. "After the first guy, Elroy Ruiz, everyone looked directly at the camera. It could be because they saw or heard a drone."

"I like the idea of a drone taking video," Lula said. "A drone's like a miniature alien spaceship, only you could get it on Amazon."

I stepped away from the computer. I didn't like looking at the videos. It made my stomach feel icky. I wanted to find the men and see them return to their normal routines. I wanted to know that they were healthy. And I didn't want them dead.

Please, please, please, I thought. Let them all be okay. And let this all be over soon. The protect-Stephanie routine was getting old.

We left the bonds office and drove the short distance to Morelli's house. His brother Anthony was sitting on the front step when we parked. He had a lumpy white garbage bag with him.

Morelli tried to squelch a grimace but wasn't entirely successful. "Looks like Anthony got kicked out of his house again."

Anthony got kicked out of his house all the time. Sometimes his wife even divorced him, but they always remarried.

"I think Anthony likes getting kicked out of his house," I said. "He drinks beer and shoots pool with you, and doesn't have to take care of his kids."

Every time Anthony got kicked out, he returned to have make-up sex, and nine months later his wife popped out another kid. It was like Darlene Boot and her chickens, except it was Anthony and his kids, running around feral in the unmowed grass around his house.

He stood and smiled when he saw us.

"Yo," Anthony said.

"Yo," Morelli answered.

This was Morelli man-speak. No more was necessary. We all trooped in and said hello to Bob.

"Now what?" I asked Morelli.

"You take Bob for a walk, and I'll fire up the grill."

"Aren't you afraid someone will snatch me?"

"You aren't associated with the diner anymore, and you have Bob to protect you."

Bob was sitting in the kitchen licking his privates. I wasn't sure how much good Bob was going to be as a guard dog.

"And I'm sure Ranger tracks your every move," Morelli said. "You've probably got GPS in your shoes, your underwear, and woven into your hair."

I hooked Bob up and walked him for almost an hour. I returned to the house, and the Morelli boys were playing billiards.

I looked out the back door. Nothing cooking on the grill. I looked around the kitchen. No burgers sitting on the counter, waiting to get eaten.

"What about dinner?" I asked.

"I dialed dinner," Morelli said. "Someone borrowed my propane."

"Are you sure someone didn't *steal* it?" I asked.

"It was me," Anthony said. "I took it last week and forgot to tell him."

I filled Bob's bowl with dog kibble, got a beer out of the fridge, and Richie Schmidt walked in with our Pino's order. Morelli and I went to school with Richie. He married Morelli's cousin Doris, and he's part of the poker night crowd. He's an electrician, but he moonlights doing Pino's deliveries a couple times a week.

"I got a chicken parm and two meatball subs," Richie said. "Looks like someone got thrown out of the house again."

"I'm not good at the marriage thing," Anthony said. "I keep having these indiscretions."

I rolled my eyes so far back into my head I almost fell over. Anthony had a good heart, and he was a charming guy, but he would hit on anything that moved and had a vagina. I wasn't even sure if the vagina was a requirement.

"Grab a beer," Anthony said to Richie. "The game's going to come on right away."

If I asked Morelli to get rid of the guys, he'd do it in a heartbeat. Truth is, I was happy to have them in his house, helping with my getaway.

I ate a meatball sub and finished my beer. Richie was at the pool table cueing up, and Anthony had the game on Morelli's big flat screen. Morelli came over and wrapped an arm around me.

"Do you want me to get rid of these idiots?" he asked.

"No. I'm glad they're here because I have to leave. I need to get back to my apartment. I miss Rex and my pillow."

"Will you come back tomorrow?"

"No, but you can come to my house."

"Can I bring my own pillow?" Morelli asked.

"You can bring whatever you want."

"Deal."

Morelli kissed me, and I had a moment of reconsidering.

"I like having you here," Morelli said.

"And I like being here, but I need space. I need my life to be normal."

"Cupcake, it's going to take more than a couple hours alone in your apartment for your life to be normal."

"I guess there's all kinds of normal."

■ ■ ■

Morelli drove me home and walked me to my door.

"I could stay," he said.

"What about Richie and Anthony?"

"They won't miss me. Richie will go home after the game, and Anthony will fall asleep on the couch. I'll call him at nine-thirty and tell him to give Bob a bathroom break."

"Would you be staying because you think I need protection?"

"No. I'd be staying because I don't want to watch the game with Richie and Anthony, and because I want to get naked with you. And then after I get naked I want to . . ."

I pulled Morelli inside before he could finish the sentence. Mr. Macko across the hall was known to crank his hearing aid up and listen at the door. He was ninety-three. I didn't want him to go into A-fib from listening to Morelli's plans for the night.

# CHAPTER TWENTY-ONE

IT WAS DARK in my bedroom with just a sliver of light shining under my bathroom door. I was naked and tangled in the sheet. Morelli wasn't next to me, and I was cold without his body heat. I pushed my hair off my face so I could see the time. Five o'clock. He came out of the bathroom, fully dressed. He kissed me on my shoulder and covered me with the quilt.

"Gotta go," he said.

"Unh." It was all I could manage.

Morelli got energized after sex. I relaxed into mush.

"How do you do it?" I asked him.

"You inspire me."

"Nice," I said.

And I meant it. It was a really nice answer. It was also true that it didn't take much to get Morelli inspired.

■ ■ ■

I waited for the sun to come up before I set my feet on the floor. I showered and got dressed and went to the kitchen. I texted Mrs. Delgado that I was home and didn't need her to look in on Rex. I made coffee and ate cereal out of the box. My apartment wasn't great, but it was home, and I was enjoying the luxury of returning to my routine. And I was enjoying the luxury of not having a babysitter following me around.

I looked out my living room window, down at the parking lot. A Rangeman SUV was parked beside my car. So much for independence. I gave up a sigh and told myself it could be worse. At least he wasn't sitting in my living room.

I cleaned the hamster cage, made my bed with fresh linens, and gathered the laundry to take to my parents' house. There was a laundry room in the basement of my apartment building, but it was lit by a flickering neon light, and it smelled like overused gym clothes and stagnant water. If I took my laundry to my mother, there was the added advantage of having it folded and ironed. Plus, I always got a bag of leftovers to take home with me. Half a pot roast. A chunk of chocolate cake. Five-bean salad. A bowl of pasta and red sauce with sausage. The possibilities were endless and wonderful.

I had the laundry basket in my hands, turned, and yelped when I bumped into Wulf.

"What the . . ." I said.

"We need to talk," Wulf said.

"Again?"

That got a small smile from Wulf. "This won't take long." He glanced at my laundry basket. "I see you have a full morning."

My windows were closed and locked and my door was double bolted, but here was Wulf. No point in asking how he got in. There were three men in my life who had seemingly supernatural skills when it came to getting into my apartment. Wulf, Diesel, and Ranger weren't stopped by the locks on my door. Morelli wasn't stopped by my door locks either, but that was because he had a key.

"As you know, I've been engaged by a friend to find someone," Wulf said.

"Ryan Meier."

"Yes. Ryan is my friend's son. He was in this country on a student visa. He left school, overstayed his visa, and took an illegal job working at the deli. Shortly after taking the job he disappeared."

"Leaving a shoe behind in the parking lot."

"Correct. Everyone is busy trying to solve the kidnapping mystery, looking for the kidnapper. I don't care about the kidnapper. I want to find Ryan Meier."

"Isn't it all the same?"

"Different focus. Different process. Five men are hidden somewhere, dead or alive. My focus is on finding those men. Three had already been kidnapped when I came on the scene. I watched the alley and was present for the fourth kidnapping."

"Wayne Kulicki."

"Yes."

"You could have saved him."

"I wasn't interested in saving him. I was interested in where they took him."

"And?"

"They loaded him into a van. I followed the van to the top deck of a parking garage. They off-loaded Kulicki, put him into a helicopter, and that was the last I saw of him. The stolen van was left behind. The three men in the van left with Kulicki."

"Wow. It's like a movie."

Wulf smiled. "Yes. I like when there's some drama involved in a crime."

"Did you recognize any of the men?"

"Victor Waggle. It was dark and they were all wearing hoodies, but there was a moment on the roof when Waggle's hood was blown off by the rotor wash."

"I'm surprised you know Victor Waggle."

"The trail goes from Ernie Sitz to Leonard Skoogie to Victor Waggle. There are others involved, but I haven't identified them. I'm telling you this because it's gone cold. Every time I had a good lead, either the police or Ranger bungled in and it went away. And now you've eliminated the deli."

"I had nothing to do with that fire!"

"You're a magnet for disaster. You're also inept but lucky. And at this point I need some luck. Hanging out in the deli, waiting for someone to snatch you, didn't work. You need to go proactive. I think the five men are still alive, but that could change if the principals panic."

"Do you have any suggestions on the proactive thing?"

"Just be your usual annoying, bumbling self. Leonard Skoogie is dead, so he's not going to be any help. There's a good possibility that Ernie Sitz is back in the country, but I haven't seen him. You should go after Waggle."

"I've tried."

"Try harder."

"What about you? What are you going to be doing?"

"I'll be watching you."

"Great. Just what I need. One more man watching my every move. Did you see them take Hal?" I asked Wulf.

"No. I missed that one."

"Had to be a big helicopter to take him away."

"Yes," Wulf said. "Something that could airlift a tank."

Ranger called just as I was getting ready to leave for laundry drop-off and office check-in.

"The fire marshal has cleared us to get into the deli building," Ranger said. "I'll meet you there in half an hour."

"Do you think it's necessary for me to walk through?"

"Yes. You're still the manager."

I made a quick detour to my parents' house. I grabbed a cheese Danish from the bakery box on the counter in my mom's kitchen, filled my travel mug with fresh coffee, and headed for the deli. Ranger was already there.

The sidewalk in front of the deli was still cordoned off with crime scene tape. The debris from the fire hadn't yet been cleared away. The brick front was stained with black soot, and the windows were boarded up. The front door was open.

I parked and walked over to Ranger. He was wearing black rubber boots and a Rangeman ball cap. He had boots and a hat for me.

"Tell me about Wulf while you change your shoes," he said.

"The Rangeman guy in the car saw him?"

"No. He got picked up by the camera over your door in the hall."

"What, no sound?"

"It only picks up sound in the hall."

I swapped out my shoes for the boots, and put the hat on. "Wulf is after his friend's kid, Ryan Meier. He was the third manager to get kidnapped. Wulf said the trail goes from Sitz to Skoogie to Victor Waggle. When the deli burned down the trail went cold for him, so he wants me to hang myself out there and go after Waggle. He said he saw the Kulicki kidnapping. Three men in hoodies loaded Kulicki into a stolen van, drove to the top of a parking garage, loaded Kulicki into a helicopter, and took off with him."

"That sounds overly dramatic. And expensive."

"It may or may not be true," I said.

"Anything else from Wulf?"

"Nope. That was it . . . other than mentioning that you're a bungler."

"It's nice to be acknowledged," Ranger said. "Let's go inside."

There was light from the open front and back doors, but the kitchen area was in total darkness. Ranger switched on a wide-beam flashlight and swept the beam across the area. I've investigated fire scenes before, so I knew what to expect. That didn't lessen the impact any. The destruction was frightening and depressing. The interior was charred black. Soot-stained water puddled on the floor and streaked across the stainless-steel appliances. A knife survived. Number seventeen on the dinner menu didn't.

We'd been told to follow the crime scene tape that ran front to back and not to stray. Parts of the floor had been marked as unsafe.

We walked the hall to the back door, looking in at the pantry and the walk-in fridge. We stepped out into the sunshine and sucked in fresh air.

"Did any of your cameras survive the fire?" I asked.

"I have one across the alley, attached to the building on the next street. The rest were destroyed."

"Did any of them catch a drone?"

"We saw one cross the lot when Hal was taken. It's probably what lured him out of camera range."

"Is there a cellar under this building?" I asked.

"No cellar. Just a crawl space with a dirt floor. I've already checked it out. Nothing interesting down there."

"There doesn't seem to be anything interesting up here either."

"I didn't expect there'd be any surprises," Ranger said. "I'm hoping we get lucky on the second floor."

"Is it safe to go up there?"

"The second deck is concrete. It's a fire floor. I'm told the damage upstairs is minimal compared to the deli."

"How do we get up there?"

"It has its own side entrance. I noticed it when I took the alley to move the car last night."

I followed Ranger to the side door and waited while he ripped the crime scene tape off and worked his magic on the police-installed padlock.

The stairs were narrow and smelled like wet dog and smoke. Once we were out of the stairwell, the air got better. There were two rooms and a bathroom. The front room had an apartment kitchen at one end. The rest of the room was filled with water-logged furniture, a couple metal file cabinets, soggy rugs that had been rolled, a metal desk and desk chair, and a medium-size safe. The second room was unfurnished, but filled with empty vegetable crates, stacks of chipped plates, a garbage bag filled with soiled napkins, and other assorted treasures.

"Can you get in the safe?" I asked Ranger.

"I'm not a safe expert," he said. "I'll text Slick."

"You have someone working for you named Slick?"

"He's an independent contractor. He calls himself Slick, and he gets paid in cash. I don't ask questions."

We each took a file cabinet and methodically went drawer by drawer.

"I'm not finding anything helpful," I said. "There's an entire drawer of appliance instructions and warranties. I don't imagine any of it covers grease fire. And there's a drawer of Ernie's income tax returns from twenty years ago."

It was a four-drawer file cabinet. I began paging through the third drawer and realized I was looking at movie and television scripts. I pulled them out and stacked them on the desk. I went to the last drawer and found folders labeled STORY IDEAS, PILOTS, CONTACTS, FUTURE PROJECTS. The folders were empty.

"What do you make of this?" I said to Ranger.

Ranger looked through the scripts. "These look like real scripts from movies and television shows."

"Why would you have a whole file drawer of other people's scripts?"

"If you had aspirations of writing or even producing you might want to study scripts that already made it to the screen."

"And what about the empty folders?"

"They're not pristine," Ranger said. "I'm guessing they had material in them, and the material has been removed."

"Did you find anything in your cabinet?"

"Papers from divorce settlements. Veterinary records for two dogs. Lease agreements for cars. Lease agreements for commercial properties. Nothing current."

There were footsteps on the stairs, and a slim older man wearing a small black nylon backpack came into the room.

"You didn't tell me to wear boots," he said to Ranger. "It's a mess out there."

"I'll include an allowance for shoes," Ranger said.

"Nikes," the man said. "Two hundred bucks."

Ranger nodded at the safe.

Slick set his backpack on the floor and squatted in front of the safe. Ten minutes later, the safe was open, and Slick took his backpack and left.

"That was disappointing," I said to Ranger. "No dynamite. He didn't even do any drilling. He just used an electronic gizmo."

Ranger opened the door wide, and we looked in. A small spiral notepad. Several bundles of hundred-dollar bills. A Smith & Wesson .38. Very similar to the gun I sometimes carried. A passport.

Neither of us moved for a beat. Ranger showed nothing, but I know my eyebrows were raised. I'm not sure what I expected to find, but it wasn't this. Ernie Sitz might have walked away from twenty-year-old tax returns and a collection of sitcom scripts, but he wouldn't have left this much money in a building he no longer owned. That left Harry or Vinnie. Vinnie didn't have this kind of money. Harry had varied interests and probably had money and fake passports stashed all over the place.

Ranger took the passport and paged through it.

"Ernest Jingle," he said.

"Is it a fake?"

"Yep. And not a very good one."

Ranger returned the passport to the safe, took out the notepad, and flipped pages.

"And?" I asked.

"Financial transactions."

He showed me a page with numbers.

"Offshore banking?" I asked.

"Bitcoin," Ranger said.

"Anything else in the notepad?"

"That's it."

He used his phone to take a picture of the Bitcoin numbers, and he replaced the notepad. The bundles of money were left.

"That's a lot of money," I said.

Ranger examined one of the bundles. "It's movie money. It's a prop."

"The gun looks real," I said.

Ranger tossed the fake money into the safe and partially closed the door. There were footsteps on the stairs, and Morelli and a uniform walked into the room.

"Looks like Krut is still sick," Ranger said.

"Pneumonia," Morelli said. "I think he's faking it so I have to take over as primary on this."

"There's a lot of faking going on," Ranger said. "The safe is full of fake things."

Morelli glanced over. "I saw Slick on the street. I appreciate that you left this open for me. I wouldn't have cause to break in, and even if I did, Slick isn't in my budget."

Ranger and I left, and Morelli stayed.

"I have to get back to Rangeman," Ranger said.

I put my shoes on, and gave him my boots. "I'm going to the bonds office. I have some loose ends."

"Victor Waggle?"

"For starters."

"Did you tell Morelli about your conversation with Wulf?" Ranger asked.

"No. I thought it would just muddy the water. He'd have yet another useless lock put on my door. And he's already got everyone looking for Waggle."

"Babe," Ranger said, giving my ponytail a playful tug.

I drove away from the deli with my Rangeman escort close behind. Don't look, I told myself. Pretend he isn't there. Ignore him.

I parked in front of the bonds office, and he parked behind me. I got out of my car, and he beeped and waved. I gave him a little wave back.

"Who's on your bumper today?" Lula asked when I walked in.

"I don't know. They all look the same. They're completely interchangeable."

"You sound like Miss Cranky," Lula said.

"The escort thing is getting old."

My phone rang, and I looked at the screen. Holy cow. It was Annie Gurky's number.

"Hello," I said. "This is Stephanie."

"This is Annie Gurky," she said. "I'm thinking that I might want to check in with the judge about my misunderstanding."

"That's great. I can help with that."

"I have a small problem that I have to take care of first. It's my cat, Miss Muffy. I want her back."

"Okay."

"And you need to get her for me."

Not okay.

"I have it all figured out," Annie said. "My scumbag, philandering ex-husband and his whore, who happens to be my ex-sister, are in Atlantic City for a cornhole tournament. They won't be back until tomorrow, so I thought this would be the perfect time for you to get Miss Muffy."

"Why can't *you* get Miss Muffy?"

"I tried. I can't get into their house. It's all locked up. I could see Miss Muffy through the window, meowing at me. Poor thing."

"I understand that you love Miss Muffy," I said, "but I can't break into someone's house to steal their cat."

"She's not *their* cat. She's *my* cat."

"It's considered breaking and entering and robbery," I said.

"They catnapped Miss Muffy. They took her when I wasn't home."

"Don't you lock your house?"

"The scumbag had a key."

"How about if I come pick you up and take you to the

courthouse to get rescheduled? Then we can find a way to get Miss Muffy back."

"No. First, I get Miss Muffy, and then I'll go with you. I've done some research. All you have to do is go to the door and holler that you're a bounty hunter and you're sure a felon is hiding out in the house. Then you can legally break the door down and get my cat."

Technically that was sort of true.

"I'm not that kind of bounty hunter," I said. "I don't break doors down."

"These are desperate times," Annie said. "You have my phone number, and I'm going to text you the address. It's easy to recognize Miss Muffy because she's fluffy. And she's a cat. There should be a cat carrier by the back door. I could see it through the window. Just put Miss Muffy in the carrier. She's very sweet."

I hung up, and my phone dinged with the texted address.

"What was that about?" Lula asked.

"Annie Gurky wants me to steal her cat back for her."

"That's a worthy cause," Lula said. "That's righteous."

"It's a felony."

"Not for us," Lula said. "We go in looking for Annie, and we can't help if the cat follows us out."

Connie had her hands over her ears. "I'm not hearing any of this."

Half Connie's family is mob. She grew up knowing when not to listen.

"It's my understanding from last time we talked to Annie that her husband has the cat," Lula said. "Does this intervention involve getting the husband out of the house?"

"The house is empty," I said. "The husband is at a cornhole competition in Atlantic City."

"Say what?"

"Cornhole competition. That's what Annie told me."

"That sounds like something sick," Lula said. "What kind of a person would participate in a cornhole competition? I personally wouldn't be involved in anything to do with cornholes. Even when I was working as a 'ho I didn't touch cornholes."

"It's a game with beanbags," Connie said. "There's a board with a hole in it, and you throw the beanbags and try to get them through the hole."

"Then why's it called a cornhole competition?" Lula asked. "Why isn't it a beanbag competition?"

"I don't know," Connie said. "I got nothing."

"So where does this guy live?" Lula asked.

"Hamilton Township."

"We should go take a look," Lula said, settling her faux Vuitton tote onto her shoulder. "Scope it out. It could coincide with lunch at the new diner on Route 33. I understand they serve an excellent Taylor's pork roll sandwich."

We took Lula's Firebird and followed her GPS to Freestone Street. It was a neighborhood of nicely maintained single-family houses. Lots were just the right size to have a swing set in the back for the kids and a fenced yard for the dog. Sidewalks were shaded by mature trees. No graffiti. No bullet holes in the aluminum siding. Very respectable. Didn't seem appropriate for the scumbag cat snatcher and his whore.

"This is a real nice neighborhood," Lula said. "I bet they got stainless appliances in these kitchens."

"We're looking for number 3625 Freestone," I said. "It's the ranch just ahead on the right."

Lula idled in front of the house. "Not a lot of bushes around it," she said. "And the neighbors' houses are close on both sides. People are going to see us creeping around, looking to break in."

"We want to go in through the back door," I said. "That's where the cat carrier is located."

"I'm thinking we do this at night," Lula said. "It's harder to see me at night on account of I'm like a shadow then. I'm like Super Dark Shadow Girl."

I was like Super White Moonbeam, but I could tamp it down if I wore a black hoodie.

Lula cruised on down the street, and the Rangeman guy followed close behind. We stopped at the diner and invited the Rangeman guy to join us for lunch, but he declined.

"He looks like he eats granola bars made out of tree bark and beetles," Lula said. "And I bet he goes commando."

The commando remark required a moment of silence from both of us while we enjoyed the mental image. At the end of the moment we gave up a sigh and ordered Taylor's pork roll sandwiches with cheese and a side of fries.

"Now that I've been a part of the food industry I'm seeing a lot of things differently," Lula said. "These forks and knives we got don't even have food stuck to them. That's a sign of a superior establishment. And the plates that are coming out are all attractive with pickles as a garnish. It's nice to have something green on the plate besides the sliced turkey."

I nodded in agreement. The grease fire was an act of God. It would only have been a matter of time before we poisoned someone if the deli had stayed open.

"Wulf dropped in this morning," I said. "He thinks I should be concentrating more on finding the kidnap victims than on trying to find the kidnapper."

"I agree with that, but I don't know how you do it. It's not like anyone left a forwarding address."

"He thinks I should try harder to capture Waggle."

"You'll have your chance tomorrow night," Lula said. "He'll be at the Snake Pit."

"He'd be crazy to perform."

"What's your point?" Lula asked.

Lula was right. Victor Waggle was a crazy man.

"I'm taking Ranger with me this time," I said.

"Don't think you're leaving me out. I got body armor and a new wig, so when my hair gets shot it's not mine."

Our food arrived, and I ate on autopilot while I thought about my conversation with Wulf. He said the connection went from Sitz to Skoogie to Waggle. The kidnappings had been caught on video and put on YouTube. The safe and the file cabinets had been filled with television and movie stuff. It was like this whole bizarre horror was entertainment . . . like reality television, or dinner theater, or a personal diversion.

I called Ranger.

"I'd like to go back to Skoogie's office," I said. "Can you get me in?"

"When you're done with lunch, have Carl bring you around to the garage entrance. I'll meet you there."

"Carl is the guy who's been following me around?"

"Yes."

Ranger disconnected, and I dug into my rice pudding.

"Why are you going back to Skoogie's office?" Lula asked.

"I went through the deli building this morning with Ranger, and there were some files missing from a file cabinet. I want to see if they're in Skoogie's office."

# CHAPTER TWENTY-TWO

LULA WENT BACK to the office, and Carl took me to the Hamilton Building, where I transferred from the Rangeman SUV to Ranger's Porsche 911 Turbo.

"Let me guess," Ranger said. "You want to look for the missing files."

I narrowed my eyes at him. "Am I wired? You heard me talking to Lula, right?"

"Wrong. I had the same thought. There's a theatrical connection between Sitz, Skoogie, and Waggle, and possibly a criminal one. I wouldn't mind seeing what's in the missing files."

"For instance, maybe under FUTURE PROJECTS would be a plan for kidnapping five men and leaving a shoe behind."

"It's an interesting hook," Ranger said.

We parked and took the stairs to the second floor. Ranger opened the door to Skoogie's office, startling Miriam. She was at her desk, looking lost.

"I wasn't sure you'd be here," I said to Miriam.

"It turns out, the business doesn't stop with death. There are contracts in place, and new deals in progress, and checks to write. It's all very confusing, because I don't seem to be working for anyone. I thought about leaving a message on the answering machine that Mr. Skoogie is dead and the agency is closed, but it felt irresponsible."

"Did Mr. Skoogie have business partners?" I asked.

"He had joint ventures," Miriam said. "It's common practice for multiple production companies to participate in a project. As far as I know the agency was solely owned by Mr. Skoogie. I suppose someone will inherit it, but I can't imagine it continuing without Mr. Skoogie."

"We're going to look around," I said. "We won't be long."

"Take your time. It's nice to have the company. It's creepy being alone in here now."

I took the desk, Ranger took the file cabinet, and we both came up empty.

"Nothing," I said. "No missing files."

"Did the police take anything out of the office?" I asked Miriam.

"No," she said. "Not to my knowledge."

"I've reviewed the security tape again," Ranger said. "Skoogie entered the building with a messenger bag hung from his shoulder. I don't see a messenger bag here. I also don't see a computer on Skoogie's desk."

"He worked on a laptop," Miriam said. "A MacBook Air. He carried it in his messenger bag. It was so he could work from home or on the road."

"Did you back it up for him?" Ranger asked. "I didn't see an external backup drive."

"He was very private about those things," Miriam said. "He might have used the cloud."

"Was he on the road a lot?" I asked.

"When I first started working for him he would occasionally travel with a band. For the past year he's been going to L.A., trying to sell a television show."

"Do you know anything about the show?"

"Not really. I've never been involved in the creative side of the business. My title is 'assistant to Mr. Skoogie,' but I'm mostly just a receptionist, and I do a little bookkeeping. I know Victor was involved. And a Canadian company was interested in producing. I believe Mr. Skoogie was trying to find a second production company with deeper pockets. And on this last trip he scheduled a meeting with a woman from HBO. Mr. Skoogie was very excited about that. I don't know how it turned out."

"What about Ernie Sitz?" I asked. "Was he involved?"

"He was very involved in the beginning," Miriam said, "but he developed some legal problems, and he disappeared. I heard a rumor that he was in South America."

We left Miriam and returned to Ranger's Porsche.

"Now what?" I said.

"Now we visit Skoogie's condo."

"Are we still looking for the missing files?"

"Missing files, missing computer, missing phone."

"Maybe they're all in the missing messenger bag," I said. "And that probably was taken by whoever came up the back stairs and visited Skoogie before Waggle found him."

Leonard Skoogie lived in a budget-friendly five-story condo building north of the government complex. We took the elevator to the fourth floor, and as we walked down the hall, I wondered if any of his neighbors even knew of his passing. The building felt impersonal.

Ranger knocked twice and announced himself. No answer. He picked the lock and opened the door.

I looked around and thought this is the way a marginally successful man lives after paying off three ex-wives. Small dated kitchen, combined living and dining room, one bedroom and one bathroom. The furniture was inexpensive and utilitarian. The exception to this was a large, elaborately carved mahogany desk that occupied the area designed for a dining table. I suspected this was the one piece of furniture he'd kept from the divorce settlements.

We searched the condo, and came to the desk last. The top was a mess of loose papers, sticky pad notes, takeout menus, and candy bar wrappers. There was a charger and cleared space for a computer. The loose papers and notes weren't helpful. A reminder of a haircut. A band contract. A party invitation. Drawers contained the usual assortment of paper clips, pens, antacids, rubber bands. The file drawer was devoted to pornography. I suppose the pornography was less expensive than acquiring a fourth wife.

"I don't see an external backup, but he has six flash drives," Ranger said, pocketing the drives. "Let's hope we get lucky."

We left the condo and drove back to Rangeman. Ranger plugged the drives into his computer, and the third one contained several short videos. There was an interior of the diner with Raymond, Stretch, and Dalia at work. The camera panned to a third man. I knew from photos that this was the first kidnapped manager. The video that followed was of the manager taking the garbage out. This was one of the YouTube videos. The next video is dark with a spotlight on the manager's face. He has a number tattooed on his forehead. He's unresponsive. The next video is Waggle with a meat cleaver in his hand. He's making chopping motions, and he looks completely insane. The last video is back at the diner and Dalia is serving a customer. The camera pans in, and we see what appears to be a penis in a hotdog bun.

Ranger pulled the flash drive out of the computer. "This answers some of our questions," Ranger said.

It took several beats for me to find my voice. "Do you think it's real?" I whispered.

"Probably not." Ranger grinned. "The size is optimistic."

"The size is *frightening*," I said. "The whole series of videos is frightening."

Ranger ran through the remaining flash drives. Two were empty and one contained two short videos of Waggle taking the money and the passport out of the safe.

When I first saw the videos of the five men being kidnapped I thought they were the product of a freak who wanted to brag about his crime. Now I was thinking the snippets I saw today might be made by a freak who wanted to show he was a videographer.

People working in a diner. People mysteriously disappearing from the diner. Crazy meat cleaver guy chopping. People's parts returning to the diner. The crazy meat cleaver guy withdrawing his money and passport and presumably getting out of town.

Not necessarily a movie I'd want to see. I was more a rom-com, sitcom, and cartoon kind of person.

Ranger put the six drives in his top drawer, pushed his chair back, and stood.

"Are you going to share the drives with the police?" I asked.

"I'm going to return them to Skoogie's desk later tonight. The police are on their own to find them. Would you like to ride along?"

"I can't. Lula and I have a job to do."

"Does it involve waiting tables and making sandwiches?"

"No! I'm helping someone with pet transport."

We were in Ranger's fifth-floor office with the door closed.

The office was small and private, and Ranger was very close. He leaned into me, I took one step back, and I was against the wall.

"I could work around the pet transport," he said.

I meant to say no, but it sounded more like *"mmmm"* when it came out of my mouth.

Ranger kissed me, and it was electric. ZING! The heat went from my lips to my toes and hit all the good spots in between. His hands slowly slid over my body, finding their way under my knit shirt.

"We should move this upstairs," he said.

"Um," I said.

"Um?"

"Here's the thing . . ."

"I hate when you start an explanation like that," Ranger said. "It's never good news."

"Kissing is cheating a little. I can deal with it. If we go upstairs it's going to be cheating big-time."

"Someday when we have more time, we need to discuss your moral compass and its reluctance to always point north."

"My moral compass is fine until you tamper with it."

"Babe," Ranger said.

Carl drove me back to the bonds office. I retrieved my car and drove to my apartment building with Carl on my back bumper. I wanted to tell him that it wasn't necessary for him to sit in my lot and wait for God-knows-what to happen, but I knew that was pointless. Carl took his orders from Ranger.

I had a bowl of cereal for dinner, and I texted Annie Gurky. I told her the pickup was set for tonight, and I would call her when it was completed. She texted back that she was very appreciative and would be waiting to hear. It was followed by a bunch of emojis. Hearts, happy faces blowing kisses, happy cat faces, hands clapping.

"Don't worry," I said to Rex. "This will be a piece of cake, and then I'll come home and we'll have a nice quiet evening together."

Rex was burrowed in his soup can house, but I'm pretty sure he was listening.

# CHAPTER TWENTY-THREE

LULA KNOCKED ON my door at nine o'clock.

"I'm all ready to go," she said. "I got on my night-stalker clothes. I'm even wearing sneakers."

She was wearing a black satin hoodie with HOT MAMA embroidered in pink on the back, a black sequined bustier, black tights stretched to the breaking point, and sneakers covered with silver glitter.

I was wearing a black Nike sweatshirt, a black T-shirt, jeans, and red sneakers.

"There's a Rangeman SUV sitting in the parking lot next to your car," Lula said. "I'm thinking as long as we can't get rid of him we might as well use him as our wheelman. Be easier for us to make our getaway with him waiting for us."

Lula had a point. I didn't expect problems, but it might be a smoother operation with a dedicated driver.

We trooped down to the lot, and I looked in at the Rangeman guy.

"You're not Carl," I said.

"Carl went off duty. I'm Eugene. I'll be with you for the rest of the night."

"I have to pick up a cat for someone," I said. "Would you mind driving us? It would make things easier."

"Of course," Eugene said.

Lula and I settled ourselves into the SUV, and I gave Eugene the address.

"I hope we're doing the right thing," I said to Lula.

"Of course, we're doing the right thing," Lula said. "We're reuniting a mama and her kitty. We're bringing poor Miss Muffy home where she belongs."

"Let's review the plan," I said. "We quietly go to the back door. We get the door open, find the kitty, and put her in the carrier that's left by the door. Then we calmly return to Eugene and drive off."

"Yep, that's the plan," Lula said. "I got my door-unlocking tools with me, too, so we won't have to kick it in."

Eugene cruised down Freestone Street. It was strictly residential, and the street was traffic free at this time of night. Lights were on in most houses. Everything was quiet.

The scumbag's house was dark. Eugene parked in front and cut his lights. Lula and I got out and quickly walked around the house to the back door.

"Do you think you can get this open?" I asked Lula.

"No problem," Lula said. "Easy-peasy."

She took a flathead screwdriver out of her purse and stuck it into the lock.

"All you gotta do is point this down a little and turn it." She jiggled it around, but it wouldn't turn.

"Hunh," Lula said. "It looked easy on YouTube."

She tried a paper clip and a nail file next. Still nothing. "This is real annoying," Lula said. She took a hammer out of her purse, whacked the doorknob, and it popped off.

Crap! "You broke their doorknob."

"That's what you gotta do when there's a tricky lock," Lula said.

The door swung open, and we stepped inside.

"What's that beeping?" Lula asked. "Do you hear it?"

I froze in place. "It's an alarm system! We activated their alarm!"

"I don't remember Annie saying anything about an alarm."

The beeping stopped and a split second later the alarm siren started wailing.

"Yow!" Lula said, holding her ears. "That's freaking loud."

A fat cat streaked into the kitchen and hunkered down under the small table. I grabbed it and looked around for the carrier. No carrier.

"Screw the carrier," Lula said. "There's going to be police here any minute."

The cat was hissing and squirming, trying to bite and claw me, trying to get away. I held it at arm's length, and ran out the door.

"Get the doorknob," I said to Lula. "Stick it back in and try to close the door. Maybe no one will notice."

I ran around the house with the cat. I could hear Lula huffing and puffing behind me.

"Start the car!" Lula yelled at Eugene. "Start the car!"

We jumped into the car, and Eugene sped away.

The cat's tail was totally bristled out, its eyes were slitty, and it was growling.

"I thought Annie said this was a nice cat," Lula said, squeezing herself against the door, getting as far away from the cat as possible. "This is the cat from hell, and I feel a allergic reaction coming on."

"It's just had a traumatic experience," I said. "We should talk to it in soothing tones. Nice kitty," I crooned at the beast.

"Where are we going?" Eugene asked.

"Pull into a parking lot somewhere, so we can make a phone call and reorganize."

Eugene found a 7-Eleven a couple blocks from the scumbag's house and parked off to one side. The cat had quieted down enough for me to loosen my grip and punch Annie's number into my phone.

"We have her," I said to Annie. "We have Miss Muffy. Where are you?"

"How do I know you really have her?" Annie said. "I want to see a picture. Maybe you could FaceTime her."

I hit the FaceTime button and pointed the phone camera at the cat.

"That's not Miss Muffy," Annie said.

*"What?"*

"Miss Muffy is a fat fluffy white cat with a pink collar. You have the wrong cat. You have a fluffy orange cat."

"Maybe it turned orange while it was away," Lula said. "Maybe someone took it to Lateesha for beautification."

"Is it possible that the scumbag has two cats?" I said to Annie.

"I suppose, but I didn't see a second cat when I was snooping around. I just saw Muffy and her carrier."

"I couldn't find the carrier," I said. "It wasn't by the door."

The was a moment of silence. "Are you sure you were in the right house?" Annie said. "3635 Freestone?"

"You told me 3625 Freestone. You texted it to me."

"My finger must have hit the wrong key," Annie said. "I've had a lot of stress in my life lately. Sometimes my hand shakes."

"Maybe it's from all that orange juice," Lula said. "Maybe you should get your liver enzymes checked."

"And now, as if I don't have enough stress, I still don't have my Miss Muffy," Annie said.

"You can have *this* cat," I said. "It's a really nice cat." Only a couple of the scratches on my arm were still bleeding.

"No! I want Miss Muffy."

"I'll get back to you," I told Annie.

"I'm not liking the way that conversation went," Lula said.

"We have to return this cat."

"No way," Lula said.

Eugene was watching me in the rearview mirror. I think he was smiling. "Are we going back to Freestone?" he asked.

I blew out a sigh. "Yes."

A solitary police car was parked in front of 3625. The interior light was on in the car, and the cop looked like he was writing a report. The light went off, and the car drove away.

I got out of the Rangeman SUV with the cat and walked to the back of 3625. I opened the back door and set the cat down in the kitchen. It hissed and tried to slash me one last time, but I jumped away. I closed the door as best as I could and returned to the SUV.

"How'd that go?" Lula asked.

"Great," I said. "The cat thanked me, and said it was sorry it scratched me."

"We still going to try to get Miss Muffy?"

"Yes."

Eugene drove to the next block and parked in front of 3635.

"Do you need help?" he asked me.

"Are you any good at opening doors?"

"Yes, ma'am," he said.

"Then I need help."

We all walked around to the back of the house and tried the

back door. Locked. Eugene took a slim tool from a pocket on his cargo pants and unlocked the door. Everyone held their breath when I opened it. No beeping. No wailing sirens. I looked down and found the cat carrier exactly where it was supposed to be.

"Now all we need is a fluffy white cat," I said.

Eugene took a penlight out of another cargo pants pocket and flashed it around the room. A white cat trotted into the kitchen and meowed at us. I scooped the cat up and zipped it into the carrier.

"Just like I told you," Lula said. "Easy-peasy."

I FaceTimed Annie from the back seat of the SUV.

"It's Miss Muffy!" Annie said. "You did it! You got Miss Muffy! I'm staying with a friend on Apple Street, just off Hamilton Avenue. I'll be waiting on the front porch for you."

We delivered Miss Muffy to Annie, and she promised to check in with the court first thing in the morning. I told her I would pick her up at ten o'clock. I thought chances were about fifty-fifty that she would be there when I arrived.

Once again, the key to true happiness is lowered expectations.

Ranger called just as we were approaching my building's parking lot.

"Babe," he said, "you're not going to make the cut as a cat wrangler."

"The second attempt went okay."

"I have part of the first one on video from Eugene's dashcam.

I'm going to save it for those days when I need something to smile about."

"Always happy to make you smile."

"Wulf is in your apartment," Ranger said. "Would you like Eugene to remove him?"

"No. He's harmless."

"He's not harmless. I'm not even sure he's human. He shows up as a blur on my video feed. He's rogue even by my standards."

"He might know something that we don't."

"Have Eugene wait in the hall, and leave your door open."

"Okeydokey," I said, but the line was already dead.

I told Lula I'd meet up with her in the office in the morning, and Eugene and I trooped upstairs. Wulf was waiting for me in my living room, standing by the window.

"We have to talk," I said to Wulf.

He smiled. "I'm listening."

"I hate when you break in like this. Stop it."

"I'll take it under consideration," Wulf said. "Is there anything else?"

"No. That's it."

"Nothing to share?"

"Nope."

"You've been busy," Wulf said. "Spinning your wheels in Skoogie's office. I could have told you it was clean."

"And the house?" I said.

Wulf shrugged.

Now it was my turn to smile. "You never searched his house," I said.

"That was an error on my part. Still, I trust you didn't find anything significant."

"Not significant."

"Mildly important?" he asked.

"Nothing worth mentioning," I said.

"Are you playing with me?"

"Not intentionally."

He had crossed the room, and he was standing very close to me.

"I could suggest a game," he said.

"I bet. No thank you. Maybe some other time."

He touched the back of my hand with his fingertip, and I felt a burning sensation. I looked down and saw that a blister was forming where he'd touched.

"How did you do that?" I asked.

"Magic," he said. "Would you like to see what else I can do?"

*"Eugene!"* I yelled.

Eugene walked in from the hall, and Wulf gave his head a small shake. "Disappointing," he said. "I expected foolish self-reliance from you."

"Are you going to disappear in a puff of smoke?" I asked him.

"No," he said. "We've had enough theatrics for one night."

Wulf left, and Eugene turned to me. "Would you like me to stay in the hall?"

"Not necessary," I said. "The Rangeman control room monitors my hall. They'll let you know if Wulf returns."

I said good night to Eugene, and I locked my door. I had a brief conversation with Rex about the state of my life. I put some first-aid cream on my burn. I made a short phone call to Morelli. And I took my MacBook Air to bed with me and watched two episodes of *House Hunters International* before falling asleep.

# CHAPTER TWENTY-FOUR

MY FIRST THOUGHT when I woke up was that it was Thursday, and I was going to have to go back to the Snake Pit. Maybe I'd get lucky, I told myself, and there'd be a cataclysmic ending of the world before Rockin' Armpits took the stage. I was kidding, of course, because a cataclysmic ending of the world would be bad. On the positive side of the morning, Wulf wasn't in my kitchen brewing coffee and scrambling eggs.

An hour later I rolled into the office. Lula had already snarfed up the best donut, and Connie was paging through a Costco flyer.

"How'd it go yesterday?" Connie asked. "Did you turn up anything new with Ranger?"

"We went to Skoogie's house and found some short videos.

If you put them all together they sort of told a story. It started with a normal day at the deli with Stretch and Raymond, and it moved on to the kidnappings, the forehead tattoo, Victor Waggle with a meat cleaver, and then it returned to the deli with someone getting served what looked like a penis in a hot dog bun."

"A penis in a hot dog bun," Lula said. "That's sick. Did it fill the whole bun?"

"Yes."

"That's a good-size penis. What about condiments?"

"There weren't any."

"Hunh," Lula said. "Everybody knows it's all about the condiments. Who wants to eat a naked penis? If I'd been on the sandwich station that penis would have had mustard and relish on it, at the very least. Or it could have been a chili dog penis. Mustard and chili and chopped onion. That's the way to serve a penis."

Connie and I exchanged glances. We didn't know where to go with this.

"Um, it's a penis," I finally said.

"All the same," Lula said. "I'm just sayin'."

"What's on the schedule for today?" Connie asked.

"I'm picking Annie Gurky up at ten o'clock. I'll let you know when I have her in custody, and you can meet us at the courthouse. I have to get my laundry from my mother. And Lula and I should check on chicken farmer Darren Boot."

"And tonight, we get to go after Victor Waggle," Lula said. "We can scope things out ahead of time when we look in on Boot."

"Do we have a full profile on Leonard Skoogie?" I asked Connie. "We know about his office and his condo. Does he own any other property?"

Connie ran him through her system and shook her head. "His wives have picked him clean."

"What about Ernie Sitz? Does he have any hidden real estate?"

"He has a house in the Burg. His wife is in it. She's filed for divorce. He has a couple properties in Colombia. Everyone assumes he's hanging out there now. He had a warehouse in an industrial park in Cherry Hill. It was foreclosed and sold at auction a year ago. That's all of it."

I knew about the house and Colombian holdings. That information had been in my original file.

"Just a thought," I said. "The five kidnap victims are being held somewhere. It would be nice to discover property owned by Sitz or Skoogie that was previously overlooked."

"I can dig around," Connie said.

Lula looked out the front window. "Who's following us around today?"

"Carl," I said. "He's working the day shift."

"Doesn't seem like there's much danger lurking out there anymore," Lula said. "Not that I'm opposed to a good-looking man riding on my bumper, but an armed guard doesn't seem so necessary."

I glanced at the burn on my hand and thought about Waggle and the meat cleaver, and an armed guard seemed like an okay idea to me.

"It's almost ten o'clock," I said. "Let's see if Annie Gurky is ready to get rebonded."

"Do you want to drive, or do you want me driving?" Lula asked.

"Carl is driving," I said. "We're going to use the Rangeman car."

Annie was waiting on her friend's porch. She was wearing a pale blue dress with a matching cardigan sweater. Her short hair was nicely styled, and she had a touch of pink lipstick. She was carrying a small purse, and she was holding a round tin.

She got into the back seat, and she gave me the tin. "My friend Dolly and I baked you some cookies this morning. It was so nice of you to get Miss Muffy for me. She slept on the pillow next to me last night. It was wonderful."

I called Connie and told her we were on our way.

"We're going to check you in at the police station and walk you over to the courthouse," I said. "Connie will meet you there and get you rebonded. After she bonds you out, she'll take you back to Dolly's house."

"That's perfect," Annie said. "I'm in a much better place

now. I have my Miss Muffy. I've changed the locks on my house. And Dolly said she would adopt Miss Muffy if I have to go away to prison for a long time."

"I'm sure that's not going to be necessary," I said.

An hour later Lula and I were back in the Rangeman SUV.

"That was real nice of her to make us cookies," Lula said, taking a cookie out of the tin. "Chocolate chip. My favorite."

I gave Darren Boot's address to Carl and told him to do a slow cruise past the Snake Pit.

"Hold on here," Lula said. "I know this taste. I've had this cookie before. It's got a edible in it. These are Hashy Smashies. They're a controlled-substance tasty treat. This cookie could put you in a real good mood, but if you eat too many of them you want to stay close to a bathroom."

I took the cookie tin from Lula and put it in the cargo area behind the rear seat.

"I'm not one to judge," Lula said, "but seems to me Annie Gurky's coping methods bear some examination. She should take up yoga or learn to play the saxophone."

There was no sign of life on the Snake Pit block. It was eerily quiet. The landscape was depressing. The area beyond it was even worse. We approached the junkyard and it was like a ray of sunshine. The big electro-magnet was working, moving cars to the smashing machine.

"I wouldn't mind working here," Lula said. "I like smashing things."

A half mile later we turned into Darren Boot's driveway.

"His pickup truck is parked in front of the house," I said to Lula. "That's a good sign."

A chicken flew out of the tall grass, flapping and squawking. It crashed into the Rangeman windshield and lay on the hood momentarily stunned. It got up, pooped, and flapped away.

"That's it for me," Lula said. "There's no way I'm getting out of this vehicle. Call Boot on the phone and tell him we're parked and waiting for him."

I dialed Boot's number. "He's not picking up," I said. "I'm going in."

"You could take Carl with you," Lula said.

Taking Carl with me had some appeal. Leaving Lula alone in the car had *no* appeal. In the past, Lula has sometimes decided she needed nachos and forgot she was supposed to wait for me.

"Carl can stay here," I said. "Darren won't be a problem."

I kept my eyes on the path and made it to the house without getting pecked. Minnie Mouse answered and invited me in.

"Darren is out back," she said. "He's working on the food truck."

"I didn't know you had a food truck."

"Goodness, yes. It uses up the excess eggs and it brings in a nice amount of money. Just go through the kitchen and out the back door."

Darren was a slim man with thinning brown hair and a large Captain Hook nose. He was hosing down a food truck that looked like a refugee from the junkyard.

"Howdy," he said. "I'll be with you in a minute. I just gotta get this washed off. The chickens make a terrible mess of it."

"What do you sell?" I asked him.

"Breakfast burritos, mostly. We don't sell them for breakfast, but they're called that on account of we fill them with scrambled eggs. When you got a night of hard drugs and drinking there's nothing better than a breakfast burrito. People stand in line forever for our burritos."

It suddenly clicked in my head. "I saw this truck at the Snake Pit," I said.

"Yep. That's where we sell them. Every Thursday and Friday night. We're famous because the big star of Rockin' Armpits, Victor Waggle, won't go onstage until he's had one of our burritos. It's a ritual for him. He shows up around ten o'clock. The security people bring him around to the back side of the truck so he doesn't get mobbed." Darren turned the hose off. "I guess you came to take me back to jail."

"Yes. You missed your court date."

"It's hard to keep track of things like that. Problem is, this isn't a good time for me. I'd appreciate it if you could come back in a couple days. I already bought the tortillas for tonight, and I'm in eggs up to my ears. And I don't know what'll happen if Victor doesn't get his burrito."

"If we go now, court is in session, and I can get you rebonded and back home for dinner."

"I guess that would be okay."

I loaded Darren into the back seat of the Rangeman SUV, and called Connie.

"We have to get him bonded out today," I said. "He has to be working on his food truck tonight."

How good is this, I thought. I know exactly where Victor Waggle will be at ten o'clock. I can have everyone in place to make a capture with a minimum amount of fuss. We'll get Waggle in cuffs, and hopefully he'll know where the kidnap victims are being held.

It was late afternoon when we went before the judge and the paperwork was completed. Lula returned to the office with Connie, and Carl and I took Darren home.

"This turned out to be a real relaxing day," Darren said. "It's not often I get to sit around and do nothing. I'm usually collecting eggs or feeding chickens or selling eggs or feeding eggs or selling chickens or . . ."

I was sitting in the front next to Carl, and I checked Darren out in the rearview mirror.

"Are you okay back there?" I asked.

"I'm freaking fine," Darren said. "Why wouldn't I be fine? I'm in this nice car and you even have bottled water and cookies back here for me. And by the way these cookies taste a little funny, but I like them anyway. They're freaking fine."

I swiveled around and looked at him. "Cookies?"

"Yep. The ones in the tin. I ate them all. I hope that was okay."

"Omigod," I said to Carl. "He ate the Hashy Smashies."

"I don't know from personal experience," Carl said, "but I hear the edibles stay with you for a longer time than just smoking weed. And they aren't always well tolerated."

"I feel a little sick," Darren said.

I squelched a grimace, and told Carl to drive faster.

"Maybe I'm just hungry," Darren said. "Are there any more cookies?"

"No!"

We had to detour around the Snake Pit. A flatbed was off-loading two giant spotlights. Vendors were finding their assigned spots on the street. Several black Escalades were lined up on the far end of the block.

Carl blew past the junkyard, turned into Darren's driveway, and skidded to a stop. I ran around and got Darren out of the car. He took two steps and projectile vomited half-digested Hashy Smashies.

"Do you think he'll be okay now?" I asked Carl.

Carl shrugged. "Were there a lot of cookies in the tin?"

"Yes."

"Bummer."

I got Darren into the house, and Mrs. Boot helped me stretch him out on the couch. A chicken immediately jumped up and settled itself on Darren's chest.

"That's Bobby Sunflower," Mrs. Boot said. "She's a cuddler."

"Darren ate some cookies that might not have agreed with him," I told Mrs. Boot.

"He has a sensitive stomach," Mrs. Boot said. "I'm sure he'll be okay if he just rests a little."

Carl was standing at the front door. "There's a lot of chickens in here," he said. "A lot of chickens."

"I don't feel good," Darren said, "but I don't care. Sometimes you have to feel bad to feel good. Have you ever noticed that?"

"Can you OD on cookies?" I asked Carl.

"Doubtful," he said. "And he lost half of them."

"Do you think he's going to be able to drive the food truck?"

"Doubtful again."

"Maybe you could drive it," Mrs. Boot said to Carl.

"I'd like to help, but I'm going off duty at seven o'clock, and I have to be back at Rangeman."

"Is someone coming to replace you?" I asked.

"Jamil."

"I don't know him."

"He's good, but he's a city boy. He might not be comfortable with the chickens."

"Tell him to pick Lula up on the way and bring her here."

# CHAPTER TWENTY-FIVE

THE FOOD TRUCK was packed with eggs and ready to go by seven o'clock, but it was without a driver. Darren was alternately dozing, rushing to the bathroom, or ranting nonsense. Mrs. Boot didn't have a license and didn't know how to drive the truck.

Lula and Jamil were parked next to Carl's SUV. They'd made a couple feeble attempts to get to the house, but had been beaten back by the chickens.

"Darren would be setting out right about now," Mrs. Boot said. "There's traffic when you get up close to the street fair, and if the truck isn't in its assigned spot by eight o'clock the spot will get given away."

I'd contacted Ranger and Morelli when I was at the courthouse and arranged for undercover men to be positioned around the food truck. If the food truck didn't show up, the men would still be on location to take down Waggle, but it might be messy. The food truck would make it clean.

I went out back with Mrs. Boot and looked at the truck. It was old, but it seemed straightforward. It didn't have eighteen gears and double clutches. It had the basics. Steering wheel. Brake pedal. Gas pedal. Recognizable gear shift.

"I guess I could try this," I said.

"I can go along and help," Mrs. Boot said. "I usually go with Darren."

The last thing I wanted was Darren's mom caught in the middle of a police operation.

"I'd rather you stay here and keep an eye on Darren," I said. "Lula will be there to help me."

I got a ten-minute crash course in burrito making food truck style, and an additional five minutes of parking instruction. I climbed into the truck and got behind the wheel.

"Drive carefully," Mrs. Boot said. "Try not to break too many eggs. If you follow the driveway through the tall grass, it'll take you out to the road a short distance from where your friends are parked."

The engine caught on the second try. I was cautious on the gas and eased the truck along the crude dirt driveway. I followed the ruts through the grass and stopped holding my breath when I reached the road. I met up with the two Rangeman SUVs, and Lula transferred over to the food truck.

"We're back in the food business," I said to Lula.

"It was meant to be. It's an act of God."

It didn't seem right to pin this fiasco on God, but I guess at the end of the day, he was the bottom-line guy. Or girl. Or gender-neutral entity.

I crept along the road, past the junkyard and the high-rent parking area. I followed Mrs. Boot's instructions and looked for the food truck entrance.

"This is real organized," Lula said. "Someone's put some thought to this. It's got professional-made signs, and the gang members aren't killing each other. Not yet, anyway. I suppose it's still early."

Jamil left me at the truck entrance, and my safety was transferred over to the Rangeman contingent on the inside. I handed an envelope filled with cash to the gate master, and in return I received a location number. I slowly rumbled along with my eggs and tortillas and stacks of fry pans.

"Here we go," Lula said. "Number fourteen."

I got the truck into position, and I opened the canopy.

"How are we going to do this?" Lula asked. "I didn't make burritos at the deli."

"We have a big griddle, six burners, and a warming oven. Darren's mom said it's up to us how we want to cook stuff. Darren puts everything on the griddle, but his mom likes to use the fry pans. The refried beans are in the slow cooker. There are more cans of them underneath the counter. There's only one thing on the menu, and it's always made the same unless someone doesn't want beans. This is a bare-bones burrito. You take a warm tortilla, you use this measuring cup to add scrambled eggs, you glop on some beans, and you squirt the magic secret hot sauce all over the eggs. Darren's mom says it's fresh eggs and hot sauce that keeps them coming back for more. There are a bunch of squeeze bottles of hot sauce next to the slow cooker."

"What about plates?"

"No plates. We have wrappers. They're in a stack at the end of the counter."

"I hope none of my fans are here," Lula said. "They would be real disappointed. There's no way for me to use my artistic talents."

"I guess they'll just have to settle for the hot sauce."

There was a lot of activity in the area. Most of it coming from organizers and vendors. Ranger was watching from the other side of the street. He nodded to me, and I nodded back. Morelli was standing in the shadow of the Flamin' Ribs and Hot Dogs food truck next to mine. Wulf was lurking a short distance from Ranger.

The public started trickling in at eight o'clock. The bands wouldn't start until ten, so this was a time to shop and socialize. We had our first customer a little after eight, and by nine o'clock we had people standing in line. I was on the griddle, and Lula was on the fry pans. I was soaked with sweat, and my hair looked like it had been electrocuted. It was pulled back in a ponytail, but it was total frizz with tendrils coming loose from the elastic band and sticking to my flushed, sweaty face. My only consolation was that I thought Lula looked no better.

I saw a couple cops and some Rangeman guys wander past the truck. It was good to know everyone was in place, and I was relieved of the burden of capturing Waggle.

At nine-thirty a large man with a lot of gold chains around his neck came to the truck and asked me for Victor's burrito.

"Sure," I said. "Where's Victor?"

"He's getting ready for his set."

"The owner of the truck said I was supposed to personally give the burrito to Victor."

"We're doing things different today."

"Sorry, I can't just give *anyone* Victor's burrito. You're going to have to move along. We have a line here."

The gold chains guy got on his phone and talked to someone. He looked over at me and shook his head. He looked down at his shoes. He paced around and talked some more. He hung up and came back to me.

"Victor wants his burrito," Gold Chains said. "He won't go on until he gets his burrito."

"And?"

"And either you give me the burrito, or else I'll shoot you."

"You'd shoot me over a burrito?"

"I've shot people for less."

Morelli was on his cellphone, and Ranger was meandering across the street, walking in my direction.

"Personally, I think you're just trying to cut the line," I said to Gold Chains, "but I'm going to humor you. Step back and I'll make your stupid burrito."

He took a step back, and Ranger and two of his men quietly disarmed him and removed him from the area.

Ranger returned moments later. Morelli was still in place. Lula had kicked off her shoes and was working barefoot.

"Look at me," she said. "I'm a burrito-making machine."

This was true. She was making two to my one. We had large wire baskets of eggs on the counter, and we'd already gone through one entire basket.

I felt a tap on my shoulder. I turned and was face-to-face with Victor Waggle.

"I need my burrito," he said. His eyes got wide as he recognized me. "You! I know who you are. You're a cop."

"Not exactly," I said. "I'm a bail bonds enforcement agent."

"I don't like them either," Victor said. "Where's Darren and Minnie Mouse?"

"Darren is sick," I said. "I'm helping out."

"Hey!" someone yelled. "It's Victor Waggle!"

In an instant, the truck was surrounded by a crush of fans. Ranger's men and Morelli's men were on the perimeter, trying to work their way through, and the fans weren't liking it. There was a lot of pushing and shoving. Someone threw a punch, and a fight broke out. The customers were smashed up against the truck, and the truck was rocking on its wheels.

"Get away from my truck," Lula shouted at them. "What's the matter with you people? Where are your manners?"

Someone tried to climb into the truck through the service window, and Lula threw an egg at him. It broke on his forehead and slimed down his face. A roar went up from the crowd, and I felt the truck begin to tip.

"Abandon ship!" Lula yelled.

Too late. The truck flopped over on its side, dumping eggs, beans, fry pans, and hot sauce everywhere. I went to my hands and knees, and instinctively crawled to the door.

Event security was mixed in with the police and Rangeman guys, pulling people off the truck and pitching them into the crowd.

I made it to the door and got to my feet. Victor followed. I saw the flash of a knife blade, and someone screamed. Victor grabbed me from behind, and put the knife to my neck. The blade sliced into me, and I saw a drop of blood soak into my shirt.

"No one move," Victor said. "Back off or I'll cut her head off."

Everyone froze.

"Drop your guns," Victor said.

About a hundred guns clattered to the ground.

"I'm walking out with her," Victor said. "No one even twitch because I'm not in a good mood. All I wanted was a goddamn burrito."

He pushed me forward, I heard a loud *BONK,* the knife fell out of his hand, and he crashed to the ground.

Lula stood over him, holding a fry pan. "Burrito that," she said. "And you shouldn't use the Lord's name in vain. It's not nice."

Waggle was facedown on the road. He had a big gash in the

back of his head, and he wasn't moving. An event security person flipped him over, and he opened his eyes.

"What the fuck?" Waggle said.

There were a lot of men, wearing a variety of uniforms, doing crowd control, pushing people back from the truck. Morelli cuffed Waggle and called for medical. Ranger was at my side. Someone handed him a towel, and he pressed it to my neck.

"It's not a dangerous cut," he said. "It's bleeding, but it's not deep."

I nodded. "I'm okay."

I said I was okay, but my teeth were chattering and my eyes were tearing up. A medic pushed his way through to me and examined the cut. I declined a trip to the hospital, but I got the wound cleaned and bandaged. Waggle was strapped to a stretcher and trundled into an EMS truck with a police escort.

"What's the plan?" Ranger said to Morelli. "One of us is going to have to get her cleaned up."

I looked down at myself. I was head-to-toe raw egg and refried beans.

"Your turn," Morelli said. "I have to stay with Waggle."

Ranger grinned at Morelli. "You trust me in the shower with her?"

"No. I trust *her.* Plus, it's going to take you an hour just to get the egg out of her hair, she's got eight Steri-Strips holding that cut together in place of stitches, and if I find out anything inappropriate happened in the shower I'll kill you."

"That sounds reasonable," Ranger said.

Lula was nearby, giving an interview to a local cable station.

"I don't usually have beans in my hair," she said to the woman with the microphone. "This isn't my best look."

"I'm leaving with Ranger," I said to Lula. "Jamil is waiting to drive you home."

Lula looked over and waved at Jamil. "Hey, sweetie," she said. "I'll be ready in a couple minutes."

Ranger opened the door to his apartment, and I stepped inside. Lights were low. The air was cool. I stood in the hallway and a glob of refried beans fell off my jeans onto the immaculate polished floor.

"Sorry," I said.

"Babe," Ranger said, "it's just beans."

I shucked my shoes and jeans, stripped off my T-shirt, and carefully made my way to Ranger's bathroom. I had a waterproof patch over my cut, so in theory I could shower. Under other circumstances, using Ranger's shower would be a luxury. He has limitless hot water, expensive shower gel and shampoo, and fluffy soft towels. Today it was a chore. My cut was throbbing, and the egg had dried in my hair.

Ranger cut the elastic that was holding my ponytail and turned the water on for me.

"Do you need help?" he asked.

"No," I said. "I don't want Morelli to have to kill you."

"I appreciate your concern. Let me know if you want to risk it."

Ranger left the bathroom, and I dropped my remaining clothes. I stepped into the shower and stood under the hot water until it felt like the goo in my hair was beginning to soften. I soaped up with his Bulgari Green shower gel and shampoo and rinsed off. I could still feel bits of eggshell stuck in my hair so I washed it two more times.

When I finally stumbled out of the shower I thought I smelled pretty good, but I was exhausted. I blasted my hair with the hair dryer, wrapped myself in a towel, and went to stand in the middle of Ranger's walk-in closet.

"No clothes," I said.

Ranger took one of his perfectly folded black T-shirts from the stack of black T-shirts and dropped it over my head.

"No undies," I said.

"Can't help you there," he said.

"Is my hair okay?"

He tucked a strand behind my ear. "Not an eggshell in sight."

"And the bandage on my neck?"

"It looks good. We'll change it tomorrow morning."

"You have a wonderful shower," I said.

Ranger moved me out of the closet and pointed me in the direction of the bed. "My bed is even better. And your boyfriend didn't say anything about inappropriate behavior in my bed."

# CHAPTER TWENTY-SIX

RANGER WAS STANDING beside the bed when I opened my eyes.

"Sorry to wake you," he said, "but the morning is moving on without us. Waggle is talking, and Morelli wants you to hear what he has to say."

"I haven't got any clothes."

"Ella found clothes for you. I put them in my closet. Grab something to eat and meet me in my office. We'll change your bandage and head out."

I took a fast shower, got dressed in my new clothes, and went down to the fifth floor. I made a quick trip to the break room for coffee-to-go and a breakfast sandwich, and I walked the short hall to Ranger's office.

"Did Waggle give up any information about Hal?" I asked.

"No. It doesn't sound like he was part of that piece of the

operation." Ranger peeled the big bandage off my neck and replaced it with a smaller one. "I told Morelli we'd meet him at the police station."

I took my sandwich and coffee in the car with me and finished eating seconds before Ranger parked. I took my coffee into the building with me.

Morelli was waiting in the hall for us, and led us into a small interview room. His eyes immediately went to the bandage on my neck.

"It's fine," I said. "A little sore to the touch but other than that it's good. No problems."

There was a small table with four chairs in the room. Morelli's laptop was on the table.

"How's Waggle?" I asked.

"His head wound is okay," Morelli said. "Lula chose a good fry pan. If she'd gone with the cast iron she might have killed him, and then we'd have no one to talk to."

"She's not much of a shot with a gun," I said, "but she's spot on with a fry pan."

"Beyond the head wound, the man has serious problems," Morelli said. "Some of the problems are drug related. We did a blood test at the hospital, and he's a walking pharmacy. I don't know how he functions at all. Plus, I suspect there's some underlying mental illness. Possibly bipolar. Possibly schizophrenia. He has lucid moments where we get snippets of information from him, and then he gets crazy eyes and goes off on a rant that's unintelligible. I've had two sessions with him.

One last night when we brought him in, and one this morning. I'm hoping you'll pick up something I missed."

Morelli pulled the first session up on his laptop and turned the computer, so Ranger and I could see the screen. There were the usual niceties of "What is your name?" and the waiving of a lawyer. Waggle was sitting slumped in his seat. His head was bandaged. He mumbled his answers and was asked to speak up.

"I want a burrito," he said. "I'm not going onstage until I get a burrito."

Morelli carefully explained to him that he was in a police station, and he wouldn't be going onstage.

"Does that mean I won't get a burrito?"

Morelli made a sign to someone off camera.

"We'll try to get you a burrito," Morelli said.

"Some people do yoga, but I do burrito," Waggle said.

Morelli nodded. The good cop understanding and sympathizing. "Tell me about Leonard Skoogie," Morelli said.

There was an instant change in Waggle. If he hadn't been shackled to the chair he would have been on his feet.

"I *hate* Leonard Skoogie," he said. "He was my agent, and he sold me out. I went to his office to kill him. I would have stabbed him and cut him up into tiny pieces until he looked like Skoogie confetti, but he was already dead by the time I got to him. How shitty is that? Nothing ever works out for me. I could hardly get the knife in him. It got stuck in his neck."

"Do you know who killed him?" Morelli asked.

"No, but I *hate* the bastard who got to him first. *I* wanted to kill Skoogie. There's no justice in this world."

"Yeah, bummer," Morelli said.

"He sold me out. I was supposed to star in the show. I was going to be a big television star, and he made the deal without me. He didn't die of natural causes or anything, did he? I would hate that. I hope he suffered. Did he suffer?"

"I don't know," Morelli said. "By the time I got to him he wasn't talking, and he had your knife sticking out of his neck. Why did you put him in the closet?"

"It seemed boring to leave him on the floor. People would come in and it would just be another dead guy on the floor. Having him pitch himself out of a closet is more memorable. And don't forget the shoe. Did you like the shoe on the desk? It made you think, right? It added to the plotline and brought it all together."

"Tell me about the plotline," Morelli said.

Waggle's eyes were darting around. "Where's my burrito? You promised me a burrito."

Morelli looked to someone off camera. "Do we have the burrito?"

Moments later a uniform came in holding a fast-food bag. He handed the bag to Morelli and left. Morelli opened the bag and passed it over to Waggle.

"This isn't a breakfast burrito," Waggle said. "There's no egg in this. And who made it? Bruce the Bear?"

"It's two in the morning," Morelli said. "This was the only burrito we could find."

Morelli hit the button to end the video.

"It deteriorates fast after this. It's like once something sets him off he completely loses it. He actually asked for a knife. He said he had to stab something."

"And the second interview this morning?" Ranger asked.

Morelli pulled the second interview up. Waggle was at the table, and he was jiggling his foot so hard his whole body was vibrating.

"He's strung out," I said.

Morelli nodded agreement. "We shipped him off to a state facility after this session."

"Tell me about the television show," Morelli said, sitting across the table from Waggle, leaning forward a little. Friendly.

"It was my idea," Waggle said. "I had the idea, and I wrote the script. And they stole it. It was a good idea. It was about a deli for cannibals. It started out like an ordinary deli, but they weren't making any money, so they got the idea to go gourmet niche."

He'd started out pale and agitated, but he was getting some color back in his cheeks as he talked about the show.

"They would get people to work in the deli, and then they'd capture them and butcher them and serve them to cannibals. Genius, right? And then for future shows they could put the extra captured humans up for auction, like they do in stockyards. And there could be these cannibal deli places all over the world. So, what do you think?"

"Wow," Morelli said.

"I even wrote a script for the musical," Waggle said.

The color went out of Waggle's cheeks, and his eyes lost focus. "I don't feel good," he said. "I need my meds."

"We're working on it," Morelli said. "Why did you actually kidnap people if this was just for a television show?"

"We couldn't sell the show, so we thought we'd do a reality thing and get some publicity. And it worked. Skoogie finally sold it."

"What about the people you kidnapped? Where are they?"

"I don't know. I just came in when they needed me to be in a scene. They took them to the stockyard or the slaughterhouse or something."

Waggle started to shiver, and someone came in and wrapped a blanket around him.

"Who's 'they'?" Morelli asked.

"Skoogie, and a couple guys from some South American place, and the sunshine-truck guy."

"Does the sunshine-truck guy have a name?" Morelli asked.

"I don't know his name, but he's cool," Waggle said. He looked around. "Is Jillian here? Jillian was supposed to pick me up."

"Jillian isn't here," Morelli said. "You're in police custody."

Waggle got crazy eyed. "The bitch said she'd be here."

Morelli stopped the video. "There isn't anything worth watching after this."

"This is too weird," I said. "Five men were kidnapped because someone wanted to sell a television show?"

"Six men," Morelli said. "One was returned."

"There's something missing," Ranger said. "Skoogie was a major player, but there have to be others. It seems reasonable that Ernie Sitz is involved. Or at least, *was* involved. Nobody can find him. Who else?"

"The sunshine-truck guy," I said.

Morelli looked over at me. "Did you get anything out of this? You were working at the deli."

"Sorry," I said. "Nothing jumped out at me."

"One last thing," Morelli said. "We retrieved Waggle's backpack from event security. It was mostly dirty laundry, but there was a clipping in it that you'll want to see. I have a photo of it on my phone. The original is in the evidence room. You can also pull it up online."

It was a short piece in *Variety,* dated the day before Skoogie died.

> *In an unprecedented move, Leonard Skoogie brokered a major network deal for* The Cannibal Deli, *an hour dramedy that was based on an experimental reality-based video. It's rumored that Chris Hemsworth has been signed to play the series lead.*

"Holy crap," I said. "Chris Hemsworth is amazing."

"He's also not Victor Waggle," Morelli said. "Waggle thought Skoogie was in L.A. pitching him."

"Yes, but Chris Hemsworth is *THOR*!"

"Put him in a Giants jersey, and I'll pay attention," Morelli said.

I left with Ranger. "Now what?" I asked.

"You tell me."

"I have to pick up my laundry, and I should check in with Connie."

Ranger drove to my parents' house and waited in the car while I ran inside. I grabbed my laundry basket, said goodbye to Grandma, and shoved the basket into the back of the Cayenne.

"Next stop is the office," I said.

Ranger drove out of the Burg and turned onto Hamilton. The office was a block away, and we could see that Darren's wreck of a burrito truck was parked at the curb. Connie and Lula were on the sidewalk by the truck. Ranger pulled up behind it, and we got out.

"Look at what we got here," Lula said. "Here's how you make lemonade out of lemons. Darren struck up a deal with Stretch and Raymond, and they're taking Breakfast Burritos on the road."

Stretch was behind the wheel, and Raymond looked out at me through the open window.

"We deliver," Raymond said. "That is our motto. We are in the true American spirit of chasing the dream. We are becoming big-deal entrepreneurs."

"I'm surprised the truck is still running after getting tipped over," I said.

"I guess you just can't keep a good truck down," Lula said.

"We must be off now," Raymond said. "This is prime burrito time. We are going to try our luck at the button factory."

We waved adios to the burrito truck.

"Did you get a burrito?" I asked Lula.

"Yeah," Lula said. "It was a pretty damn good burrito."

"Anything new come in for me?" I asked Connie.

"Nope. Slow morning," Connie said.

Ranger and I returned to his car, and I asked him to ride past the deli. I was thinking about Hal. I had an unrealistic but hopeful fantasy that we'd drive down the alley behind the deli, and Hal would be standing there looking confused.

Ranger cruised past the front of the deli and went around to the alley. He stopped and idled for a moment by the dumpster and the parking lot. I looked at the lot and the deli's charred back door, and I had an epiphany.

"Omigod," I said. "I know the sunshine truck. It's Central GP. It has a big sun on the side of the truck. The slogan is WE SELL EVERYTHING UNDER THE SUN. And if Vinnie was transported in it, the inside of the truck might have smelled like bananas. Frankie is the snitch who always knew when a manager was hired. He was at the deli every day."

Ranger called his control room and asked for information on Frankie and the location of the Central GP truck.

"Are you going to call Morelli?" I asked.

"Not yet. Morelli's a good cop, but he's held back by procedural rules and layers of bureaucracy. I can move faster."

This was true. It was also true that Ranger frequently operated in the gray zone of not quite legal.

We were about to pull into the Rangeman garage when Ranger's control room got back to him. Frankie's full name was Frank Russel Lugano. He lived in a second-floor apartment not far from the deli. His Uncle Constantine owned Central GP. Leonard Skoogie was his cousin on his mother's side. Frankie's live-in girlfriend was a waitress at Hooters. And Frankie didn't report in for work this morning.

"He's running," I said. "He's probably on a flight to Guatemala."

Ranger cut across town and turned onto Whitson Avenue. He drove two blocks and parked in front of Frankie's building. It was three stories. Brick. Smushed into the middle of a row of similar Practical Pig sturdy but uninteresting buildings. We took the stairs to the second floor and got there just as Frankie was leaving.

"Back it up," Ranger said to Frankie. "We'd like to talk to you."

"I'm in kind of a hurry," Frankie said.

"This won't take long," Ranger said, motioning Frankie back inside.

It was a small, nicely furnished apartment with no girlfriend in sight.

"Tell me about the kidnappings," Ranger said.

"You know as much as I do," Frankie said.

"Not true," Ranger said. "We just finished talking to Victor Waggle."

Frankie rolled his eyes and dropped the duffel bag he'd been carrying. "Waggle. I had reservations about this gig from the beginning. We all did. We knew sooner or later Waggle was going to screw it up. He's an incredible talent, and he's batshit crazy. You give him drugs to try to calm him down, and he gets even crazier. Lenny didn't want to cut him out. He had no choice."

"I'm not interested in the details," Ranger said. "I want to know where the kidnapped victims are being held."

"That's a problem," Frankie said. "I don't know where they are. I was a minor player in this fiasco. They wanted to use my truck to help make a movie. It sounded like fun. And they were going to pay me. All I had to do was show up, they'd load some guy into the back, and then I'd drive him to a pickup point. The Colombians took over from there. One time they were doing a big scene with a helicopter and I had to borrow a van to transport everyone. They thought a van was a better visual with the helicopter."

"It was okay with you that you were part of a kidnapping?" I asked.

Frankie shrugged. "Yeah. It didn't seem so bad. It wasn't like anybody was going to get hurt. It wasn't like they were going to ransom them off or anything. They just wanted to make a movie. Lenny figured he could get some publicity with the kidnappings, and he could make this reality show thing, and get people to look at it. And it worked. Was a shame he died just when he should have been celebrating. Or maybe he died because he did too much celebrating."

"Where do I find the Colombians?" Ranger asked.

"I don't know," Frankie said. "They always found me. I'd meet them in a parking lot somewhere and transfer the body. They only spoke Spanish. I never knew what they were saying."

"Who was in charge of the Colombians?" Ranger asked.

"Should I have a lawyer or something?" Frankie asked.

"We aren't police," Ranger said. "I'm just trying to find Hal."

"Okay, I get that," Frankie said. "I'd like to help you, but this started out simple and just got more and more complicated. We were only supposed to take one guy, but Lenny wasn't getting enough publicity. Nobody was watching the little movie. There's too much stuff out there on YouTube. So, Lenny kidnapped more guys and kept making bigger and better movies. You gotta give it to Lenny. He wasn't a quitter."

"The Colombians," Ranger said.

"They're just worker bees. Ernie brought them with him from his place in Bogotá."

"Ernie Sitz?"

"Yeah. Lenny's partner. It started out with Lenny and Victor. Then Lenny needed money so he brought his pal Ernie in."

"Anyone else involved?" Ranger asked.

"Harry. He came in late and funded a production company. I never met Harry, but apparently he doesn't speak Spanish and the guys from Colombia don't understand much English, and so one day Harry is on a rant because a bunch of women came to his daughter's house complaining about her husband. So, these Colombians misunderstand and snatch the husband."

I glanced over at Ranger and saw his mouth twitch into a hint of a smile.

"Vinnie?" I asked.

"I don't know the guy's name, but we had to drug him up and return him."

"Where do we find Ernie?" Ranger asked.

"He jumped ship when Victor went down. He's going back to Bogotá. I think he had a flight this morning."

I looked at the duffel sitting on the floor. "Is that where you're going?"

"No. I have a ticket for Flight 127 to Hawaii, then maybe I'll go to El Salvador. I have friends there. Gonna do some fishing."

"Have a good trip," Ranger said.

"Thanks," Frankie said. "I hope you find Hal, and he's okay. The original plan was to drug the men and send them home, but I don't know about Harry. I hear he's mob."

# CHAPTER TWENTY-SEVEN

"HOW ABOUT NOW?" I asked when we were in the car. "Do we bring Morelli in now?"

"No, but I'll have him keep Ernie off the plane."

"Are you going to let Frankie go fishing?"

"No. I'll have Morelli detain him."

Ranger drove the short distance back to Rangeman and went directly to his office. He sent Morelli a text about Ernie and Frankie, and he accessed a program on his computer that listed all assets for Ernie Sitz and Harry Hammerstein.

"Omigod," I said. "Harry's last name is Hammerstein? I never knew. I just knew him as Harry the Hammer."

Ranger limited the assets to properties within a hundred miles. Sitz had seven, and Harry had sixteen. I looked over Ranger's shoulder at the list.

"This one," I said, pointing to a building on Harry's list. "The warehouse in Cherry Hill. It was owned by Sitz and went up for auction a year ago."

Ranger went to Google maps and looked at the satellite view of the property.

"It's in an industrial park that's mostly abandoned," Ranger said. "The warehouse is off on its own. Good location to hold someone hostage. Smart. You don't want to kidnap someone and cross state lines. I think it's worth looking at."

Ranger called Tank and told him he needed two cars and four men in ten minutes.

"I'll be traveling with Stephanie," he said. "We'll need full security. Vests and belts. And I'll need a thermal drone."

Ranger and I went in his Porsche Cayenne. The other two cars were fleet SUVs. Tank was driving one of them. We took I-295 south and reached Cherry Hill midafternoon. The entrance to the industrial park wasn't gated. The warehouse Harry owned was toward the back end not quite a quarter mile down the road. Tank and the other Rangeman SUV hung back, and Ranger and I drove past the warehouse. No cars parked in the adjoining lot. No lights shining from the office windows in the front of the building. No visible activity. We parked alongside the other two Rangeman vehicles and got out.

"I want to know what's inside the warehouse on the next block," Ranger said. "Send the drone up."

One of the men opened his laptop and another removed the

drone from a box in the back of the SUV. He set the drone on the ground and in minutes it was in the air, humming its way across the parking lot. It hovered over the warehouse and sent back thermal images.

"Five men in a large room and four more in a smaller room," the guy with the laptop said.

Everyone crowded around to look at the screen.

"I'll take point," Ranger said. "Tank will watch Stephanie's back. We'll worry about the four men in the smaller room. I'm hoping the five men in the large room are our hostages. We're not sure this break-in is justified, so use restraint."

The drone returned and everyone suited up in body armor and gun belts. Tank handed me my vest and utility belt.

"Are you sure you want me along on this?" I asked Ranger.

He shrugged into his vest. "I didn't think you would want to miss it. And more important, I need you to justify the break-in. You have the papers that allow you to go after Ernie Sitz. Stay close to Tank. We're going in looking like the *RoboCop* SWAT team. I'm hoping we look serious enough to make this a nonevent."

I stuffed myself into the vest and buckled the utility belt on. It contained a flashlight, a knife, a stun gun, pepper spray, and a couple extra clips for the Glock I had strapped to my leg. It probably contained other stuff too, but I didn't look all that close.

I glanced down at the belt. "I don't see any granola bars," I said to Ranger. "And where's the kitchen sink?"

"Babe," Ranger said.

We drove across the street and parked close to the back door to the warehouse. Ranger unlocked the door, and we went in, moving quickly through the building. Ranger at point, motioning clear, the rest of us following. No one speaking. We reached a door at the end of a corridor, and we all stopped and watched Ranger. He tested the door. Not locked. He opened it and we all rushed in, guns drawn. Okay, my gun wasn't drawn, but I rushed in with everyone else.

Four men were playing cards at a small table. They all jumped up when we came in. One of them pulled a gun and immediately thought better of it, dropping the gun on the floor.

"Do you speak English?" Ranger asked.

"A little," one said with a heavy accent.

Ranger switched to Spanish. The four Rangeman guys looked like they understood everything. I understood nothing. One of the card players pointed to the door at the far side of the room. It was steel with multiple locks.

Ranger's men cuffed the card players and sat them on the floor. Ranger removed a key ring from one of them, crossed to the door, and unlocked it.

I'm not sure what I expected to see. Five emaciated men, crying with joy at being rescued. Maybe in cages. Maybe shackled.

Ranger pushed the door open, and I followed him in. The room was half the size of a basketball court. Cement floor. High ceiling. Brightly lit. Five cots with sleeping bags and pillows. A card table with four chairs. Wastebasket next to it filled with Dunkin' Donuts and Mike's Burger Place bags. Games were stacked up by the table. Monopoly, Scrabble, Trivial Pursuit, Candy Land, Axis & Allies, checkers. Large flat-screen television in front of a big leather couch. A basketball hoop had been screwed into the wall opposite the television.

Three men were watching television and two were shooting hoops. All of the men were naked. I didn't know three of the men, but Hal and Wayne Kulicki looked like they'd each gained about twenty pounds.

Hal was one of the basketball players. He cupped his hands around his privates when he saw me, and his face got red.

"This looks like Club Med for hostages," Ranger said. "All it needs is a pool and a hot tub."

"It's not that good," Hal said. "They cheaped out on the sports package for the television."

"Are you going to call Morelli now?" I asked Ranger.

"Yep," Ranger said. "Time to call Morelli."

"This is more secure than it looks," Hal said. "There's only one door. It's always locked and the men never come in alone. Always four of them with guns. We have nothing to use as a weapon. No knives or forks. They feed us burgers and donuts. There aren't any windows. The walls are concrete. We have one bathroom with a shower. No towels or toothbrushes. Makes you wonder what was originally stored here."

"Are there more guards than those four?" Ranger asked.

"There used to be eight in total," Hal said. "They would work in shifts. Three of us speak Spanish and from what we could hear through the door, four of them left to go back to Colombia yesterday. The four out there now were leaving tonight. I didn't take that as a good omen for my future."

"Do you know who's in charge of the Colombians?" Ranger asked.

"Ernie Sitz is involved. I don't know beyond him."

Ranger gave me a corporate credit card. "We passed a Target when we got off the highway. Find some clothes for the men. Pajamas, shorts, anything. Tank will drive you."

I returned forty minutes later. Local police were already at the warehouse. Morelli pulled in behind me.

"You went shopping?" Morelli asked, looking at my Target bags.

"The kidnap victims are naked. I went out to get them some clothes."

"Makes me happy," Morelli said.

I led the way to the basketball court and handed the bags over to the men. Underwear, T-shirts, sweatpants, and flip-flops.

"You're pretty casual about all these naked men," Morelli said to me.

"You've seen one and you've seen them all," I said.

"Is that true?"

"No," I said to Morelli. "Absolutely not."

Ranger joined us. "Were you able to find Sitz?" he asked Morelli.

"Yeah. We found him at Newark Airport. He was stuffed into a garbage container."

"Is he okay?" I asked.

"No," Morelli said. "He's dead. I don't know any details."

Ranger and I exchanged glances. Harry the Hammer was cleaning house. That included friends and foes and partners. He was tidying up loose ends that could tie him to the kidnappings. Classic mob behavior. There were four Colombians left behind who may or may not know anything about Harry. And there was Frankie from Central GP.

I caught a flash of black in my peripheral vision and turned to find Wulf standing a short distance away. He was in full Wulf regalia. Black cape. Black suit and dress shirt. Blood-red pocket handkerchief.

"Thank you for locating my charge," Wulf said.

He crooked his finger in a come-here gesture, and Ryan Meier ran over to him.

"Oh man," Ryan said to Wulf. "Am I ever glad to see you."

"Your father's been worried," Wulf said.

Wulf spread his arms wide, flaring his cape. There was a flash of blinding light, a crack of thunder, a lot of smoke, and when the smoke cleared, Wulf and Ryan Meier were gone.

"I didn't see that," Morelli said.

I agreed. I didn't see it either.

"I saw it," Hal said. "It was awesome."

Ranger stayed stoic, but I knew he was mentally rolling his eyes.

"I'll take Hal back with me," Ranger said to Morelli. "He'll be available if you need to talk to him."

"I'll pass that on to the feds," Morelli said. "They're about a half hour behind me with the crime lab. Not that I expect they'll find anything worthwhile here. This warehouse belongs to Harry, and Harry knows how to cover his tracks. I'm sure you already know this. We also got full disclosure on *The Cannibal Deli*. Harry is listed as an executive producer. He bought into a production company that's involved. If I'd asked my mother instead of having the department research the show, I could have found out sooner. Apparently, it's the hot gossip topic in the Burg."

"Have you talked to Harry?" Ranger asked.

"Harry is on a Caribbean cruise. He gets back tomorrow."

"Nice," Ranger said. "What about Skoogie. Any tests back?"

"Skoogie overdosed. Looks like self-inflicted and accidental."

"Kulicki needs to check in with the court," I said to Morelli. "He's my FTA. And when they pry Ernie Sitz out of the trash receptacle, he has my name on him too. He's way overdue, but Vinnie should still be able to get something back on his bond."

"I'll take care of it," Morelli said. "I'm going to be tied up here for a while. Can you walk Bob for me?"

"What about Anthony?"

"He's back home with the wife and kids."

Ranger parked in the lot behind my apartment building.

"This has been interesting," he said.

"Do you think Harry had Sitz killed?"

"Yes."

"Do you think the police will be able to prove it?"

"No. Harry will eventually get convicted of something and get sent away for a while, but I don't think it will be for Sitz. Some loyal lieutenant did Sitz. Probably Connie's Uncle Jimmy."

"He's in his nineties!"

"He's fearless. He has nothing to lose. He's too old to die young. And he works with Billy Raguzzi."

I knew Billy. I went to school with him. He was a quiet, skinny little guy. His nickname was Billy Coldcock. Also, Billy the Eye Gouger.

"Billy is taking up the trade?" I asked.

"Learning from the best," Ranger said.

I glanced over my shoulder at my laundry basket in the back seat. "I need to check on Rex and make sure nothing is fermenting in my refrigerator."

Ranger carried my laundry basket to my door and waited while I rummaged around in my bag for my key. He got tired of waiting, produced his own key, and let me into my apartment.

"Thanks," I said. "And thanks for carrying my basket, and thanks for keeping me safe. It looks like I'm not in danger anymore, so you and Morelli don't have to keep tag team guarding me."

"No more than usual," Ranger said.

He nudged me inside, set the basket on the floor, and kissed me. "I'm cutting you loose," he said, "but feel free to drop in if you get a sudden desire to use my shower or my bed."

He kissed me again with enough passion to make me think twice about his offer.

"Jeez Louise," I said.

"Babe," Ranger said. And he left.

I stood for a moment regrouping, thinking it felt good to be home. I went to the kitchen and looked into the fridge. No green slime growing on anything. I tapped on Rex's cage and said "Hello!" Rex stuck his head out, twitched his whiskers, blinked his black eyes at me, and retreated back into his soup can. This all made me feel happy inside.

I carted my laundry basket into my bedroom, brushed my hair and retied my ponytail, applied some lip gloss, and smiled at myself in the mirror.

I was about to leave for Morelli's house to walk Bob when Grandma Mazur called.

"I've got news," she said. "Don't tell your mother, but I'm running off to live in sin with my honey."

"Again?"

"It's better this time. It's not one of them Internet honey things. This is a honey from the neighborhood. We've been seeing each other at the Wednesday night viewings at the funeral home. I think this is the one. He's older than me, but he's a real looker. He's got a good job too. That's why we're going on a sexcation. He just finished a project and came into some money, so we're heading off to Atlantis."

"Do I know him?"

"Yep, just about everyone in the Burg knows him," Grandma said. "He's related to Connie, and he's a big deal in the Knights of Columbus. He wears one of them sashes to funerals and everything. It's Jimmy Rosolli."

"Don't go anywhere. I'm coming over. We have to talk."

"Well, that's the thing," Grandma said. "I'm on the plane with my honey, and we're about to take off, so I have to shut my phone down. I just wanted to make sure your mother wouldn't worry when I didn't come home, so I thought you could make up a good fib."

"*No!* I'm not fibbing for you, and you don't want to go to Atlantis with Jimmy Rosolli! Get off the plane *NOW!*"

Catch up on the latest books by

#1 *New York Times* bestselling author

# JANET EVANOVICH

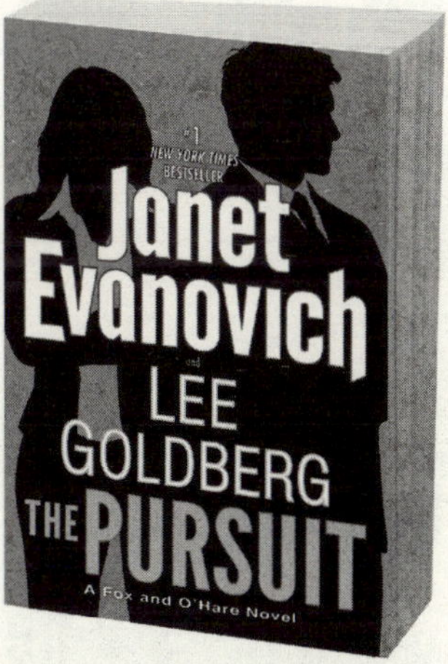


Visit EVANOVICH.COM for updates, excerpts, and much more!

# Join JANET EVANOVICH on social media!

JanetEvanovich

@janetevanovich

janetevanovich

JanetEvanovich

Visit EVANOVICH.COM and sign up for Janet's e-newsletter!